DATE DUE

GHANA

A Historical Interpretation

GHANA

A Historical
Interpretation

J. D. FAGE

GREENWOOD PRESS, PUBLISHERS
WESTPORT, CONNECTICUT

Library of Congress Cataloging in Publication Data

Fage, J. D.
    Ghana, a historical interpretation.

    Reprint. Originally published: Madison : University
of Wisconsin Press, 1959.
    Includes bibliographical references and index.
    1. Ghana--History--To 1957. I. Title.
DT511.F3 1983   966.7   83-1543
ISBN 0-313-23884-7 (lib. bdg.)

With the exception of the two maps of modern Ghana which were prepared by G. H. Adika, Dept. of Geography, Legon, all illustrations in this book were adapted from Description de l'Afrique, *a French translation from the Flemish of Olfert Dapper, printed in Amsterdam in 1686.*

Reprinted with the permission of the University of Wisconsin Press

Reprinted in 1983 by Greenwood Press
A division of Congressional Information Service, Inc.
88 Post Road West, Westport, Connecticut 06881

Printed in the United States of America

10 9 8 7 6 5 4 3 2 1

Foreword

The post of Commonwealth Visiting Professor in the field of history was created at the University of Wisconsin in 1955 to continue and extend the tradition founded by Professor Paul Knaplund. Generous support has been provided by the Thomas E. Brittingham Foundation, the Carnegie Corporation, and the Kemper K. Knapp Trust Fund. Each year a distinguished historian is invited from within the Commonwealth of Nations. During his semester at Wisconsin, he supplements the work of the resident faculty by giving a course on his own part of the Commonwealth. In addition, the visitors deliver the annual series of public lectures named in honor of Professor Knaplund, whose work over several decades has made Wisconsin a center for Commonwealth studies. So far, a Canadian, an Australian, an

Indian, and Professor John D. Fage, of the University College of Ghana, have held the post.

The lectures that follow are the Paul Knaplund Lectures for 1956–57, delivered in April and May of 1957, only a few weeks after the formal entrance of Ghana into full independence and membership in the Commonwealth. It was a peculiarly appropriate time for a historian to reinterpret the history of the Gold Coast in the light of its emergence as the independent nation of Ghana. This kind of reassessment is one that historians must constantly carry out. The movement of history brings forward new political, economic, and social conditions. It is part of the historian's function to explain why these changes have taken place. New events constantly bring forth new questions about the past, and the historian is driven back to the record of the past in search of new answers. As a result, the body of historical knowledge has a variable, rather than a fixed, content.

The field of Commonwealth history, and particularly that of the British Empire and Commonwealth in Africa, has been one of the most rapidly changing of all historical fields in recent decades. A bare half-century ago it was taken for granted that "history" was the study of the history of "civilization," and civilization in turn stood for an accepted line of development from the ancient Near East to Greece and Rome, through medieval Europe, and on to the achievements of nineteenth-century Europe and America. The rest of the world was left to a handful of "Orientalists," and "the East" in common understanding stood for all of that vast variety of civilizations and cultures that have flourished to the east or the south of the Mediterranean. It was much the same as the ancient Greek concept of "the barbarians." If these countries had a history at all, it was taken to be a history without substance and without meaning for the modern world.

With the two world wars and the rise of Asian countries to independence, there has been a reëvaluation. Since the historians' business is to find out how the world came to be as it is, they were forced to look again at the history of the non-European world. First Latin America and then Asia became subjects of serious study in a way that was not true of the nineteenth century. In the world outside the West, Africa was the last important continent to receive adequate attention. As late as the 1930's, many historians believed that no history of Africa, in the sense of an account of events based on written records, was possible for the period before the European invasions of the nineteenth century. Beginning with the inter-war decades, however, and increasingly since the second World War, historians began to discover that sources for African history were much richer than many had supposed. New research began to change our whole concept of the African past, though much of the new work has only recently been published. Even today, few American universities offer undergraduate courses in the history of Africa, and American scholarship lags far behind the research of British, French, and Belgian historians of Africa—to say nothing of an emerging generation of historians in tropical Africa itself.

One of the special problems of African history is the escape from the older Europe-centered view of the world. The first investigations took account only of the exploits of Europeans in Africa, with little understanding of African culture and little or no consideration for the role of the Africans themselves. The history of the British Empire in Africa was only the history of British activities, but this is now changing with the realization that the imperial power, in Africa or anywhere else, did not operate in a vacuum. The local culture and tradition, and local individuals, must be taken into account, not merely as background for the impact of Western culture and European rule, but as an important and integral part of history.

Much of the newer work in Commonwealth history has moved away from the older tradition of concentration on central policy, as it has moved away from the older concentration on political and constitutional history. It is no longer centered one-sidedly on European expansion, nor yet concerned solely with local affairs. What used to be called the "imperial factor" is still very important, and sometimes decisive, but it can no longer hold its place as the central factor of colonial history. It was, after all, only one item in a complex web of political and cultural interrelations between the colonial people—in this case the Ghanaians —and the West—in this case not only the British but the Portuguese and Dutch as well.

Another new dimension is a greater depth in time. As long as the history of the Commonwealth was merely the history of British activity, there was no need to go back beyond the period of British control. For most of modern Ghana, this would mean beginning the account with the twentieth century. As Professor Fage's study makes clear, modern Ghana is not simply a product of the twentieth century. Its emergence depends on a long and complex interaction between Europe and Africa, and on an even longer development within Africa itself.

PHILIP D. CURTIN

Preface

During the second semester of 1956–57, I had the privilege and pleasure of serving in the Department of History in the University of Wisconsin as visiting Professor in the history of the British Commonwealth, an appointment made possible by the generosity of the Thomas E. Brittingham Foundation and the Carnegie Corporation, and which carried with it a share of the onus of continuing in the tradition of Commonwealth Studies so notably maintained at Madison for so many years by Professor Paul A. Knaplund. My primary responsibility was to conduct courses in the history of the British in Africa, but I found that the visiting Professor was also expected to give a series of public lectures. At the time that I was to give these lectures, the African territory of the British Commonwealth in which I have been working for the last nine years was just on the point of advancing from colonial status to that of a dominion, a free and independent nation of the British Commonwealth, a change which was accomplished on March 6, 1957, when the colony of the Gold Coast became the new state of Ghana. It therefore seemed appropriate to attempt to present to my American audience something of the historical background of the new state, to try and place the history of the territory and its people in some kind of meaningful relationship with the histories of Africa and of European and of British expansion into Africa. These lectures, with some modification, form the contents of this book.

When I went to lecture at Madison, it was the Gold Coast that I left; when I returned from Madison to Africa, the land to which I returned had become Ghana. Nevertheless it has seemed advisable to retain the old name of Gold Coast for most of this written version of the lectures. The lectures are historical, ending with the emergence of modern Ghana, and for a large part of the period with which they deal the only general name for the area of West Africa with which they are concerned was the Gold Coast. Secondly, the words Gold Coast have a precise geographical sense as a name for a particular stretch of the West African coastlands, and the retention of this name should serve to avoid the risk of confusion which might otherwise arise in the minds of some readers from the fact that the new Ghana has taken its name and national inspiration from the ancient empire that once existed in the western Sudan, an empire which is also touched on in the present book.

The title under which the lectures were given was "Ghana, the Gold Coast, and Africa," but this was a title determined by the circumstances of 1957. The present title will, I trust, make clear what I think will be obvious enough to readers acquainted with any part of the great expanse of ground and of time which I have endeavoured to encompass, that there is little claim to originality in this work. My aim throughout has been to achieve a historical perspective for both ancient and modern Ghana (and for the old Gold Coast). If I have in any measure succeeded, it must be principally because I have succeeded in understanding what other people have discovered and have made known, either in their published work, or in the course of personal discussion or correspondence. Acknowledgement of the first category of sources is made in the notes; the second category is far more elusive, but I would like especially to thank Professor Philip Curtin, Mr. Thomas Hodgkin, Mr. David Kimble, and Mr. G. E. Metcalfe for their kindness in reading and commenting on the manuscript before publication.

J. D. F.

Legon, Ghana
May, 1958

Contents

GHANA

A Historical Interpretation

CHAPTER I

The African Background

The boundaries of the new Ghana at its birth were those of the old British colony of the Gold Coast together with British-mandated Togoland, and are essentially artificial in the sense that they do not correspond with any well-marked ethnic or geographical divisions. They arose as the result of the piecemeal extension of British rule northwards from the Gulf of Guinea into the West African interior. Until well on in the nineteenth century, the term "Gold Coast" meant literally a coast, a stretch of the shore of the Gulf of Guinea extending from about the mouth of the river Tano in the west to about the mouth of the river Volta in the east, a coast to which Europeans first came in the fifteenth century to trade for gold and on which they established trading posts which, in the seventeenth and eighteenth centuries, were primarily concerned with the export of slaves to the American continent. After, and to some extent as a consequence of, the campaign against the slave trade during the earlier part of the nineteenth century, British influence was gradually extended over the small African states of this coast, and the influence of other European peoples declined, processes which culminated in 1874 in the proclamation of the Gold Coast as a British colony. The limits of this colony were not precisely defined, but in general terms it may be said to have been effective along the coast from the Tano to about fifty miles east of the mouth of the Volta, a distance of about three hundred miles, and northwards into the interior for an average depth of perhaps fifty miles.

In 1896, the powerful military kingdom of Ashanti, immediately to the north of the Gold Coast, whose nineteenth-century expansion had been a constant source of trouble both to the native states and to the Europeans on the coast, was forced to submit to British protection. This brought British influence a further 260 miles into the interior. The development was confirmed and extended in 1902, when Ashanti became a colony directly under British rule and its hinterland for a further 150 miles northwards was constituted the Northern Territories Protectorate. Finally, after its conquest by British and French forces during 1914–18, the German colony of Togoland, which had been established in the 1880's and 1890's immediately to the east of the three British territories, was divided between the conquerors, and in 1922 the western and smaller zone was entrusted to Britain by the League of Nations as a mandated territory to be administered integrally with the Gold Coast territories.

In terms of political geography, then, the British colony of the Gold Coast finally took shape in the early years of the twentieth century as a rectangular slice of West Africa with its major axis running inland for some four hundred miles at right angles to the Guinea coast in about 1° W. longitude. This rectangle cuts directly across the principal geographical divisions of West Africa, which run parallel to the sea and are due basically to the gradual decrease of rainfall, from the coast, in about 5° N. latitude, towards the Sahara desert, which begins in about latitude 17° N.

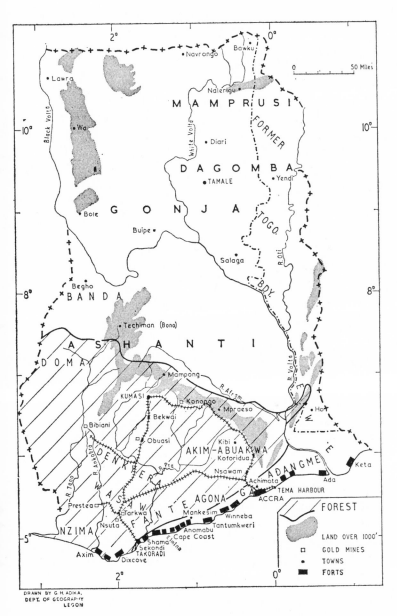

Modern Ghana

The wettest part of the country is in fact the extreme south-west, which receives eighty or more inches of rain a year. A hundred miles from the sea, in southern Ashanti, annual rainfall still averages as much as sixty inches. The greater part of the southern half of the country is, as a consequence of such rainfall, covered with dense tropical forest. As latitude increases, northern Ashanti and the Northern Territories receive progressively less rainfall so that the forest gives way to open woodland, and this in its turn is succeeded by grassland savanna. However, the northern boundary of the Northern Territories, in 11° N. latitude, comes appreciably short of anything approaching desert conditions, receiving a rainfall of about thirty inches a year.

The area of tropical forest forms a triangle with its greatest depth in the west, where it reaches to the coast. In the east the forest tails off to an apex some thirty miles from the sea at a point where the Volta, the major river system of the country, draining its entire northern half, cuts through the Akwapim-Togoland range of hills, which run across the southern part of the country from southwest to northeast. Between these hills and the coast lie the Accra plains, a triangular area of comparatively dry open grassland receiving an average of thirty or less inches of rain a year.

There are alternating wet and dry seasons, the former extending over the months between March and November in the forest zone, and being concentrated in July, August, and September in the savanna country of the north. Temperatures are nowhere significantly modified by altitude since the highest land, to be found in the Akwapim-Togo hills, rarely exceeds two thousand feet above sea level. In the southern half of the country, mean temperatures throughout the year lie within the range 70°–85° F., with mean relative humidities of the order of 70 per cent; in the north, the range of mean temperature is approximately 75°–95° F., and mean relative humidities are around 50 per cent. [1]

The people of the country are all of Negro stock, with little significant variation in physical appearance. Two major ethnic groupings may, however, be distinguished. These are most clearly apparent in terms of linguistic classification. All the indigenous languages spoken in the Gold Coast belong to the West Sudanic family of African Negro languages, but whereas the languages of the peoples of the south, that is of the pre-1902 Gold Coast colony, of Ashanti, and of the southern districts of Togoland, form part of the subfamily which linguists call the Kwa languages, those of the Northern Territories and northern Togoland are part of the Gur subfamily. Kwa languages are spoken throughout West Africa, south of about latitude 9°, from the Niger in the east to about Liberia in the west; the Gur languages, as their alternative and older name, Voltaic, implies, are spoken principally in the area contained within the great bend of the river Niger which is drained by the Volta and its tributaries. It will be appreciated that the area in which Kwa languages are spoken corresponds almost exactly, in that part of West Africa in which the Gold Coast or modern Ghana is situated, with the region which is typically covered with thick forest. We may say, in effect, that the Kwa languages are the languages of the peoples inhabiting the major central block of the West African forest lands, whereas the Gur group of languages is one of the major subfamilies of Sudanic languages employed by the people of the West African savanna or Sudan.[2]

The boundaries of the Gold Coast colony created by the British, and hence of its successor state, the new Ghana, thus not only cut across a major geographical division of West Africa, that between forest and savanna, but also across a major ethnical division. The distinction between the Negroes of the forest and coast on the one hand, and the Negroes of the savanna country between the forest and the desert on the other hand, is fundamental to an understanding of the history of the peoples of the Gold Coast, and indeed of West Africa generally. To the historian, the distinction would not appear essentially cultural, although of course it is neatly marked by language, one of the important expressional delineations of culture. In the West African forest and savanna alike, the foundations of cultural and political organisations are essentially the same and essentially Negro; the cultural differences that may be seen would seem to be largely the result of adaptations to different environments. To the eyes of an historian, the fundamental environmental fact would seem to be that, throughout history, the savanna country has always been open to access from other parts of Africa, and movement across it has always been relatively easy, especially during the long dry season, while on the other hand, until recent times—a space of less than a century—the West African forest proved extremely resistant to human movement and penetration.[3]

In its pure state, the forest is composed of great trees whose trunks, standing close together, rise from buttressed roots straight up into the air for two hundred feet or so before branching out into foliage. There is practically no direct sunlight at ground level and thus no plants to provide fodder for large cattle or transport animals; instead, giant creepers abound, presenting, together with the buttresses, an almost impenetrable obstacle to the free movement on any appreciable scale of men and their possessions. Only the advanced technologies developed during the industrial revolution of the nineteenth century could really provide keys to open up the forest, in the form first of the railway and then of the motor road. The barrier presented by the forest was furthermore greatly enhanced by the diseases communicated by its myriad insect population, of which yellow fever, malaria, and dysentery were perhaps the most lethal or debilitating for man, and trypanosomiasis for his animal auxiliaries. The understanding, treatment, and conquest of these diseases was effectively begun only during the twentieth century.

The obstacle presented to human penetration and movement by the West African forest and its diseases could not wholly cut off people living there from influences from the outside world, but it did serve to filter and to attenuate such influences during a long period of time in which the inhabitants of the savanna were in contact with movements of people, trade, and ideas which may be regarded as elements of, or as connected with, the main stream of historical development in the world around the Mediterranean. Whereas the West African forest lands have historically served as a barrier to human intercourse, the Sahara desert never seems to have fulfilled this role. It is not known for certain when men

first began to traverse the desert between North Africa and the
West African savanna, but there is evidence, in the form of rock
engravings of horse-drawn carts along at least two main north-
south routes in the western Sahara, to suggest that such traffic
goes back well into prehistoric times.[4] It might even be suggested
that trans-Saharan traffic has continued without interruption ever
since the Quaternary period when the Sahara was not desert, but
grassland supporting a considerable variety of African fauna now
found only much further to the south in wetter lands.[5]

Although in historic times the Sahara has always been a desert
(this in fact is the significance of its name, in Arabic *as-Sah'ra,*
"the waste"), it has never been wholly uninhabitable by man, and
once the camel had become accepted in Africa as a beast of bur-
den, it became possible for intercourse across the desert between
the habitable country of North Africa and that of the Sudan to
become established with considerable certainty and regularity.
At the time of the introduction of the camel into Africa from
Asia, that is to say about the beginning of the Christian era, the
desert may have been inhabited, at least in part, by Negro peoples. The evidence for this is by no means conclusive, but it is
probably safe to say that, though there were also non-Negro Mediterranean peoples in the desert, the latter had not universally
imposed their dominance.[6] But the adoption of the camel by the
Mediterranean peoples of northwest Africa—and by the fourth
century the camel was in general use as far west as Morocco for
ploughing as well as for draught purposes—gave them a weapon
which placed eventual mastery of the desert in their hands.[7] Two
consequences of this should be noted. First, the Negro frontier
was definitely pushed south across the desert into the savanna
lands of West Africa, the region now known to geographers as the
Sudan, from the Arabic term *Bilad-as-Sudan,* literally "the land
of black-skinned people." To us today, perhaps, the Sudan is not
typically the land of the Negro; we would place it further south,
in the region known generally as Guinea,[8] whose northern frontier is usually equated with the northern limits of the forest which
has historically served to protect the world of the Negroes from
undue modification by incursions or influences stemming from

Mediterranean Africa. But to the Mediterranean peoples expanding across the desert with the aid of the camel, it was the savanna which was the land of the Negro, because it was there that their expansion began to be checked by the opposition of much more dense and homogeneous Negro populations. It was in the savanna country of the Sudan, in fact, that in the terminology of logistics, the Mediterranean peoples began to come to the limit of their line of communications. There are a number of examples of North African states attempting to establish political empires on the further side of the Sahara in the Sudan—perhaps the best known are the Moroccan conquest of the Niger bend region at the end of the sixteenth century [9] and the Egyptian conquest of the Nilotic Sudan by Muhammad Ali and his successors in the nineteenth century [10]—but none achieved any permanence.

On the other hand, and this is the second point, possession of the camel by the North Africans enabled some of their tribes, particularly pastoral-nomad Berber tribes whose original habitat was the steppe lands of northwestern Africa between Tripoli and the Atlantic, to establish and control regular trade routes across the desert between North Africa and the Negro communities of the western Sudan. The existence of these Mediterranean-controlled trans-Saharan trade routes has been a factor of the greatest importance in determining the main lines of development of West African history in the pre-European period. But before considering these, and the relation to them of the peoples of what until recently was known as the Gold Coast, there are some other aspects of the conquest of the Sahara by Mediterranean people from North Africa that should be examined, if only briefly.

First of all we should notice that the southwards expansion of North Africans would appear to have been most rapid and most complete in the west, that is in the hinterland of present-day Morocco, Algeria, and Tunisia, rather than in the hinterland of Cyrenaica and Egypt. For example, in the Nile valley, predominantly Negro Christian kingdoms held out against even the Arabs and Islam until the thirteenth and fourteenth centuries,[11] while today some of the peoples of the eastern Sahara, in Tibesti and Kufra, for example, are still as much Negroid as they are Mediterranean.[12] It is as though the movement of Mediterranean expansion was one which was pivoted on Egypt and swung through its greatest distance along a western arc. At first sight this might seem odd, since the vehicles which gave this expansion its momentum both first entered Africa from the east, through Egypt.

One of these, namely the camel, has already been mentioned. The other, which we must now consider, was Islam and its propagators, the Arabs. In general terms there can be little doubt that the advent of the Arabs and Islam served further to accelerate and intensify the process of the expansion of Mediterranean peoples into the Sahara already facilitated by the camel. It seems possible also that differences between the nature of the Arab conquest of Egypt and the manner in which Islam was accepted there, and the nature of the Arab conquest and of the acceptance of Islam in North Africa west of Cyrenaica, in the lands which in Arabic are *al-Maghrib*, "the West," go some way towards explaining why the Mediterranean expansion was quicker and more thorough in the western Sahara than it was towards the east. Egypt was a land whose sedentary agricultural people were long accustomed to foreign rule; once the Byzantine armies had been defeated and the Arabs had occupied the head of the delta, the site of modern Cairo and ancient Memphis, and its major seaport, Alexandria—and this was accomplished with little difficulty in two short years (639–41 A.D.)—the land was theirs, and in course of time, almost inevitably, the people of Egypt became Islamised and even to a remarkable extent Arabised. But the conquest of the Maghrib was a protracted affair extending over several decades, if not centuries, in which Arab armies not uncommonly met defeat at the hands of Berber tribesmen proudly defiant in defence of their own independence, religion, language, and culture. It may be doubted whether the Arab conquest of the Maghrib was ever complete; certainly it cannot be accounted so before the mass invasion and settlement of the Bedouin tribes, the Bani Hilal, Bani Sulaim, and Bani Maqil, some four centuries after the first Arab incursions.[13]

Although, in the long run, the peoples of the Maghrib could not escape the dominance of Islam, Islamic culture, and the

Arabic language, many of them did not accept these things readily. Some Berber tribes found new expression for their protestant
desire for independence in the sectarian impulses of Islam.
Among these, Kharijism was too negative a principle to have outstanding political results, but Shi'ism produced first the independent ninth-century kingdom of the Idrissids, and then the Fatimids, who, turning the tables on the Arab invaders, succeeded,
towards the close of the tenth century, in extending Berber rule
to Cairo and even beyond. The Fatimid Caliphate could not retain the Maghrib, but that country then produced the successive
empires of the Almoravids and Almohads. In the eleventh and
twelfth centuries, these provided the Berber world with its most
magnificent achievements, culminating in the establishment of
one Berber rule for the whole Maghrib, including Muslim Spain.
It was not until the thirteenth century, nearly six hundred years
after the first Arab conquest, that Barbary finally succumbed to
the erosion of the Bani Hilal and similar Bedouin immigrants.

The consequences of this prolonged struggle between the Berber tribes and the Arabs for mastery in the Maghrib are undoubtedly better understood for the Maghrib itself than they are for its
Saharan borders, but enough is known to suggest that one effect
of the struggle was to incline some pastoral Berber groups to
move into and across the desert, transferring their nomadisation
or transhumance from the northern to the southern borders of the
Sahara, from the Maghribian steppes to the Sudanese savanna.[14]
The motives for emigration would in some cases be resistance to
Islam; in others, the failure of minority Muslim sectarian groups
to achieve a firm footing in the politico-religious upheavals of
contemporary North Africa. Thus the Lemta, who entered what
was to become the Songhai empire of Gao, were pagan Berbers,[15]
while the Abuyazidu or Bayajidda invaders recalled in the legends of Hausaland seem to point to the unsuccessful tenth-cen-
tury revolt against the Fatimids of the Kharijite Zenata, Abu
Yazid.[16] In one case at least, that of the *muleththemin,* the anti-
Muslim and the sectarian motives would seem to be confused.
The *muleththemin,* the veiled Berbers of the desert, produced
not only the Muslim Almoravids, one wing of which under Abu

Bakr, pushed back into the desert by the success of his cousin Ibn Tashfin in engrossing the government of Morocco, turned to the conquest of the Sudanic state of Ghana, but also the modern Tuareg tribes, whose adaptation to Islam extended over many centuries.

There are, however, other considerations besides the advent of Islam and the Arabs in the Maghrib which may help to explain why the southwards movement of Mediterranean peoples towards Negro Africa began earlier and was more pronounced in the west than was the case in the east.

Evidence of prehistoric, pre-camel routes across the Sahara has so far been revealed only in the western half of the desert. It may be that evidence of a similar kind will eventually come to light in the eastern Sahara, between the longitude of Lake Chad and the Nile. But since such evidence is not yet obvious, it is at present permissible to venture the conjecture that even before the day of the camel, or of the Arabs and Islam, there was something in western Africa which tended to draw people from North Africa across the desert more than was the case in the east.

What this was, we have no certain means of knowing, but there are a number of pointers which we might consider. The first is that from Lake Chad in the central Sudan westwards along the line of the Niger and the Senegal rivers to the Atlantic we would seem perhaps to have better conditions for the emergence of relatively developed civilisations than elsewhere in the Sudan except, perhaps, in the Nile valley. From Lake Chad westwards are to be found unusually good supplies of water to support the development of agriculture and relatively dense populations. One of the oldest West African cultures known to us, that of the Sao or So, flourished in the Chad basin itself.[17] In the same latitudes further to the west emerged the great historical states and empires of the western Sudan, from Ghana, originating perhaps about the fourth century A.D. and reaching its peak about the tenth century, through Mali and Songhai, which reached their apogee in the fourteenth and sixteenth centuries respectively, to more modern or more lasting states such as those of the Bambara and of Hausaland and Bornu.[18]

It should also be noted that the north-south width of the Sahara is narrowest between the Gulf of Sidra and Lake Chad, and between southern Morocco and the Niger bend. It is at these points that the Sudan, or Negro Africa, projects most closely towards Mediterranean Africa. Other things being equal, one might expect the transit of the Sahara to be easiest at these points, with the result that the main trade routes from North Africa would tend to flow from Morocco towards the Niger bend and from the region of Tripoli to that of Lake Chad. In fact, as we have seen, this does seem to have been the case from the days of the cart routes, revealed by the rock drawings, until the close of the era of the great camel caravans at the very end of the nineteenth century.

It must also be appreciated that the headwaters of the Senegal and Niger rivers afford alluvial gold. Gold can still be recovered here by primitive placer methods today, and though by modern standards the output is unimpressive, before the great gold strikes of the nineteenth century it must have been appreciably more important.[19] Gold, of course, has always acted as a powerful incentive for the development of trade; it could be that it was gold that drew the people of the ancient carts across the desert to the western Sudan. (It should be remembered, incidentally, that a similar magnet operated in early times in the far eastern Sudan, east of the Nile, in the gold mines of the Wadi Allaqi.[20]) It may be that the famous voyage of the Carthaginian Hanno along the west African coast in the sixth century B.C., the interpretation of which, together with that of other voyages of African exploration reported by classical authors, has occasioned a lively controversy,[21] was also in some way connected with an ancient trade to the western Sudan for gold. Such a supposition might be strengthened, though, as Bovill points out,[22] by no means confirmed, by the fact that among the Arab geographers who describe the western Sudan, Mas'udi (tenth century A.D.) and Yaqut (thirteenth century), both describe the trade with the Negroes for gold as conducted on the basis of the same "dumb barter" (silent trade) reported by Herodotus as being used by Carthaginians on the shores of Africa beyond the Straits of Gibraltar.[23]

Be this as it may, it is noteworthy that when, in the eighth century of the Christian era, the western Sudan, and in particular the empire of Ghana, first came to the notice of Arabic authors, it was at once described as a "land of gold," which suggests that gold was already an established commodity in trade between the Sudan and the Maghrib.

The earliest known Arabic reference is that of Al Fazari in the eighth century, who says no more than that Ghana was "the land of gold." In the following century, Al Yaqubi, describing the Sudan from east to west, wrote, "Finally there is the kingdom of Ghana, the king of which is very powerful. In his country there are gold mines. Under his authority are other kingdoms . . . and gold is found in all these regions." These early authors do not seem to have been strictly accurate in saying that the gold was mined actually within the kingdom. Later authorities, for example Mas'udi and Idrisi,[24] suggest that the gold-producing region, which they call Wangara, lay just outside the political control of Ghana to the south, and this view has been accepted by modern commentators such as Delafosse and Bovill who identify Wangara with the region between the river Faleme, a tributary of the Senegal, and the upper Niger.[25]

The significance of Ghana, and then successively of other great towns in the western Sudan, such as Mali, Gao, Timbuctu, and Jenne, or of the Hausa centres such as Kano and Katsina in the west-central Sudan, was that they were situated in the northern borderlands of the Sudan. They were essentially centres for Negro communities lying just beyond the limits of the effective political power of the invaders from North Africa. These limits were not of course fixed; they varied from time to time. Thus after 1076, Ghana came within the sphere of operations of the Berber Sanhaja nomad tribes who constituted the motive force behind the Almoravid movement, but in this case it is noteworthy that primacy in the western Sudan shortly passed to another Negro power further to the south, that of Mali, and that under the camel nomads the agricultural lands that had been the core of the state of Ghana became reduced to desert or near-desert. It is true also that Timbuctu started as a Berber settlement, and that traditions, which in this case are not necessarily always to be taken at their face value, assert that the founders of the first ruling dynasties of Ghana, of the Songhai empire of Gao, of Bornu, and of the Hausa states, were originally "white" men from the north whom it is sometimes possible to identify with tribes of North African origin.[26] But when Ghana, Mali, and Gao were at the height of their political power as the capitals of great empire-states, the evidence is clear that these states were essentially Negro in population and culture and that their rulers were Negroes also.

We know enough about Mali and Gao, and by inference of Ghana as well, to be able to suggest in general terms how these extensive empires arose and how their power was maintained.[27] The fundamental unit in which the Negro peoples were, and to some extent are still, organised in West Africa was a greater or smaller group of people bound together by ties of kinship, of descent from a common ancestor. The unit might be so small as to be no more than an extended family of hardly more than three generations in depth, or it might be a large and more complex structure which perhaps may best be termed a clan. Originally ultimate authority in such kinship groups would be vested in one man, usually the most suitable male descendant in the direct line from the founding ancestor, who would work with the advice and consent of the recognised elders of the group's various kinship segments. Such authority would be at once social, political, and religious in character. In a hypothetical primitive state, each kinship group would be economically self-sufficient.

Now with the approach of the Mediterranean groups from across the Sahara, men with a more complex form of society and with a more advanced material culture, represented perhaps as much by their possession and use of camels and horses as by their possession of more advanced tools and weapons, horizons would be widened and new opportunities for trade would arise. The northerners would be interested in acquiring from the Negroes gold, kola nuts, and slaves (the latter an essential feature of Mediterranean society); in exchange they could offer various kinds of manufactured goods hitherto unknown to the Negroes—cotton cloth seems to have been one of the most significant of these—

and also salt, an essential commodity of life which was scarce in the Sudan but readily obtainable from rock-salt deposits in the Sahara.[28]

It would not be unnatural if in these circumstances the idea should occur to certain Negro kinship groups that they would gain much more from their trade with the Mediterranean peoples if they could control a larger area than that actually occupied by their own people. Consequently some kinship groups began to embark on the conquest and the domination of others, and in this way states, or in some cases large empires, emerged in which political authority had to be to a great extent divorced from social authority and, in an animist society, from religious authority. This was so because it lay in the hands of one kinship group and its rulers who had no necessary kinship ties with the subject kinship groups. The process of conquest and state-building would be facilitated by military and administrative techniques acquired from contact with the Mediterranean tribes. One of the most telling of these techniques in the savanna grasslands was undoubtedly the use of cavalry. Contact might often include intermarriage between the dominant or emergent-dominant Negro clan and the leaders of the Mediterranean groups, and commonly the employment of men of Mediterranean or mixed Mediterranean and Negro descent as advisers and administrators.

The role of Islam in this process of state- and empire-building, once it had begun to reach into the western Sudan, which was from the tenth century onwards, is not unequivocally clear. In the case of Ghana and the Almoravids it was a destructive force, but this was probably an unusual case. More generally it would seem to have helped in the process of state-building by providing a valuable leaven of literate culture. Indeed some Sudanese cities, notably Timbuctu, emerged as considerable local centres of Muslim culture and scholarship. In the expansion of trade in the Sudan, as will be seen, it is quite clear that Islam played a very significant role. Arabic was valuable as a language of diplomatic communication; as a medium of commercial intercourse and accounting, Arabic, or at least Arabic script, was quite essential.

But in the fullest sense Islam was never wholly assimilated by the Negroes of the Sudan. The mass of the people preferred their own religion, culture, and way of life. This is shown in any number of ways, but one example is of particular historical interest. The principal weakness of the great Sudanese empires was the failure of their rulers to establish any valid relationship between themselves and the subject kinship groups other than the possession of superior military force, and possibly the establishment of peace and commercial prosperity over an unusually wide area, though much of the prosperity was channelled into the palaces and capital cities of the rulers, and the maintenance of peace depended on the continued military superiority of the ruling group. Such a valid relationship between rulers and ruled was almost impossible to achieve in a land where the basic ties were those of kinship, where the intercession of departed ancestors was an integral part of religious worship, and where land could really only be thought of as belonging to the descendants of ancestors who first settled and cleared it. However, some of the later Songhai kings of Gao attempted to use Islam as a new cement of empire transcending all relations based on kinship. But the result seems to have been the reverse of that looked for: namely, as M. Rouch suggests, the provocation of a strong animist and tribal reaction and the weakening and eventual disintegration of the structure of the empire.[29]

The economic role of the new states and towns in the Sudan close to the southern edge of the desert was essentially that of go-betweens in the trade between the Mediterranean and the Negro worlds. The northern merchants came to places like Ghana, Gao, Timbuctu, or the Hausa cities, and there exchanged their goods for commodities brought in by essentially Negro merchants. Some of these commodities doubtless originated within the area of political control of the rulers of these cities, but even the most extensive empires, such as Mali, stopped short of the West African forest, while the Hausa states, which were often commercially and industrially extremely important, were mostly of quite small extent. Many of the typical Sudanese exports, especially kola nuts, which are a forest crop, and probably many of the slaves and some of the gold, came from regions far to the south of the great commercial and political centres in the Sudan. But they were brought in by Sudanese merchants based in these centres, who gradually established trade routes extending ever further to the south.

The area encompassed by the former Gold Coast colony, which is entirely south of latitude 11°, was too remote from the line of great Sudanese commercial emporia ever to have been included in the great empires which waxed and waned about them. Nevertheless, by the time that Europeans first penetrated into the forest that lies behind the Gold Coast proper, that is by the early nineteenth century, it is evident that the kingdom of Ashanti was the terminus of two major trade routes from the Sudan. One led from the northwest, from the area inhabited by Mande-speaking Negroes, an area which encompasses the area of the upper Senegal and of the upper Niger down to as far as Timbuctu, and which in political terms included the great states of Ghana and Mali. This route was dominated by a caste of Mande traders, the Mande-Diula. The other led from the northeast, from Hausaland, and was controlled by Hausa traders. When the Mande and Hausa traders first reached as far south as Ashanti might not be easy to determine exactly, but they were already well established there by the nineteenth century as traders, and even as propagators of Islam—not that they had much chance of success in weaning the Ashanti, or even less strongly organised Gold Coast peoples, away from the traditional beliefs which were so essential a part of their whole way of life. Nevertheless, we should note that Joseph Dupuis, who visited Kumasi, the Ashanti capital in 1820, and who had had consular experience in North Africa, was able to converse with these traders in Arabic, and even to acquire geographical manuscripts written in Arabic.[30]

Although we can say no more of the penetration of the trade routes from the north into the Gold Coast forest than that the northern traders were already established at Kumasi by the early years of the nineteenth century, there is some dating evidence available for the establishment of trade with the north in the regions immediately north of the Ashanti forest. Trade between the ancient state of Bono (conquered by Ashanti in 1740 and incorporated in the Ashanti Union as the state of Techiman) and the northwest, in gold and also in kola nuts, is traditionally stated to have begun in the reign of the second king of Bono, whose dates as given by Mrs. Meyerowitz are 1328–63. The capital, Bono-Mansu, became a twin city, with separate Muslim and native towns.[31] This feature, of which Ghana provides an early prototype, was also found in Bono-Mansu's trading rival Begho, the capital of Banda, about seventy miles further west. By the end of the sixteenth century, the tensions implicit in such a situation, heightened by an increase of immigration from Mande country, an immigration which gave rise to the state of Gonja, caused the destruction of Begho and serious difficulties in Bono.[32]

For the northeast route, we are told that trade between Gonja and Kano (in kola nuts) began in the time of Kano's nineteenth king, whose dates as given by Palmer are 1452–63,[33] while Islam is said to have reached Dagomba, east of Gonja and to the northeast of Ashanti, in the time of King Zangina, about the end of the seventeenth century.[34] The direction from which Islam reached Dagomba is not known. It could have come through Gonja, or it could have come along the northeast trade route. If the latter, the time lag compared with the advent of Islam along the northwest route is consistent with the fact that the establishment of Islam in Hausaland was also due to the Mande and is to be dated about the fourteenth century.[35]

But though the influence of trade and of cultural propagation brought from the Sudan by Mande and Hausa merchants has been of the greatest importance in the history of the peoples within the area of the former Gold Coast colony, it is not the only link which these peoples have with the great events which we have just been considering in the lands where the Sudan merges into the desert. The most remote traditions of origin of many of these peoples suggest that the original founders of their states were emigrants from the Sudan. The mode of organisation of some of these states, especially north of the forest, would also suggest that the process of state-formation we have been reviewing also extended south towards the Gold Coast in some way,

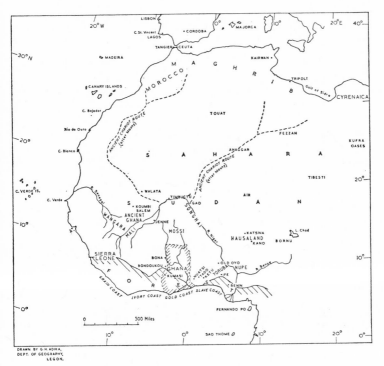

The Modern Ghana in Relation to Africa

although of course it need not necessarily have been transmitted by actual emigrants from the great Sudanese states.

We have earlier made a basic distinction between the peoples of the northern Gold Coast savanna who speak mainly Gur languages and the peoples of the Gold Coast forest speaking Kwa languages. An examination of the traditions of origin of the former is simplified by the fact that, although something like two dozen indigenous political units were eventually recognised by the British after the establishment of their government in the Northern Territories, only three of these units were of much size or consequence, namely Dagomba, Mamprussi, and Gonja, and many of the lesser units were either offshoots of Dagomba and Mamprussi or were, or had been, subject to them. The traditions of origin of the rulers of Dagomba and Mamprussi, and also of the three major Mossi states just to the north, in the French colony of the Upper Volta, point unequivocally to their ancestors having emigrated from the region of Hausaland and Lake Chad at a time which must be closely related to the period, about the eleventh century, when the Hausa states themselves were beginning to take shape. These kingdoms of the Gold Coast Sudan may thus be fairly simply classified as second-degree examples of the process of state-formation in the Saharan Sudan which we have already examined. It is permissible to conjecture that they may have been created by kinship groups that did not succeed in the struggle for trade and power further to the north, and which chose to emigrate rather than to remain as subject peoples.[36]

The case of Gonja is somewhat more complex. In the first place, it is further south than Mamprussi and Dagomba, less of a savanna state and more nearly in the forest. Secondly, when European contact was first established with Gonja, its political structure was much more in decay than was the case with Dagomba and Mamprussi, or with Ashanti and lesser states in the forest. Thirdly, although Gonja's traditional origins were more definitely expressed and much later in time, averring that the state was created by migrants from Mande-land as recently as the early seventeenth century, clearly the great majority of its people are not Mande and not overly Mande-influenced, and the language of the country is a Kwa language related to the languages of the forest. The Mande element in Gonja was obviously small and was limited to a recent and not very successful ruling element.[37] The significance of this will become apparent after some account has been given of the traditions of origin of the Kwa-speaking peoples of the country.

For the purposes of this survey, the inhabitants of the Gold Coast forest and coastlands can be divided into two groups: a smaller group concentrated in the extreme southeast, largely in the more open country between the Akwapim-Togo hills and the sea, and a larger group, the peoples speaking languages termed Akan, who inhabit the remainder of the country, the more forested part. The smaller group comprises two subgroupings, the Gã and Adangme of the Accra plains, and the Ewe of southern Togoland. Their languages are mutually unintelligible, but their social organisations are rather similar; what specifically political and military organisation they have seems to have been borrowed from their Akan neighbours;[38] and their traditions of origin indicate that both groups came to the Gold Coast from the east in a number of waves, the earliest probably arriving not earlier than about the fifteenth century.[39]

The Gã, Adangme, and Ewe traditions conform to an observable cultural and linguistic pattern, namely that the Kwa-speaking peoples are distributed about a lateral axis parallel to the coast. They would seem also to suggest that the prime centre of dispersion of this culture is in the east, among the Yoruba and the Edo, the peoples who produced the world-famous Ife and Benin brass castings. Thus the line of migration of the Ewe is remembered as Ketu-Tado-Nuatsi (Notsie); that of some of the Gã-Adangme groups ran through Nuatsi from "Same between the rivers Efa and Kpola," a location which suggests the Niger delta, while according to a Benin tradition, the Gã left there *c.* 1300.[40] Ketu is today the capital of one of the westernmost Yoruba states;[41] Tado, about sixty miles from the coast on the river Mono, was the centre of dispersion for the Adja, a people akin to the Ewe, who together with the Fon or Fõ constituted the core of the great state of Dahomey, a state much influenced by the

Yoruba; [42] Nuatsi, the modern Nuatje some fifty miles north of Lome, the port and capital of French Togoland, was the Ewe centre of dispersion. Small groups of Adangme survive as islands among the Ewe in Togoland. The Ewe name for the Gã is Gẽ, and there is a people who call themselves Gẽ in southeastern French Togoland whose language is usually classified as a dialect of Ewe. Similarly in southeastern Dahomey are the Gũ or Egun, and, according to Dr. S. O. Biobaku, the earliest Negro inhabitants recalled in Yorubaland were "probably Efa or Egun peoples." [43]

Enough has been said to demonstrate that Gã, Adangme, and Ewe traditions are consistent with the idea of the Kwa-speaking peoples developing along a coastwise axis from east to west. But the earliest traditions as yet recovered among the much larger Akan group of Kwa-speaking peoples in the Gold Coast all indicate a dispersion not from the east, but from the *north or northwest,* from the Niger valley from Timbuctu westwards, the region of development of the empires of Ghana and Mali. It is plausible to interpret traditions among the Akan, particularly in the territory of ancient Bono and modern Gonja, as indicating that their ancestors left the Niger valley at about the time when Ghana was in decline and Mali was beginning to emerge, that is to say about the twelfth century, and some confirmation of this may be seen in traditions of the upper Niger valley.[44]

The Negroes of Ghana and Mali were what we should now call Mande-speaking peoples; the word "Mali" indeed is a variant form of "Mande." [45] But the Mande languages are a subfamily of the Sudanic family of Negro languages quite distinct from the Kwa subfamily to which the Akan languages belong. Thus not only do Akan traditions run contrary to the east-west line of the other Kwa-speaking groups of the Gold Coast, but they also appear to be inconsistent with the linguistic evidence.

The impasse is more apparent than real, and a key to its solution is provided by the situation in Gonja. The Mande traditions of origin of Gonja, as has been seen, are not the traditions of the bulk of the people, but of a small ruling class which established its domination comparatively recently (c. seventeenth century), and which has not totally identified itself with the people at large. The latter in fact belong to the Kwa cultural grouping. Their language and the language of the country, Guang, is Akan, and they possess residual traditions of origin of their own, separate from those of the ruling class, which, as we have seen, can be equated with those of the Akan states. Clearly the modern state of Gonja has resulted from a comparatively small band of invaders (from Mande-land) imposing their rule on (Akan) groups already resident in the country when they arrived. Although the invaders have dropped their own language and have taken up that of the mass of the people, their conquest was too recent, and perhaps also not sufficiently positive, to result in a complete merging of the two stocks and their traditions.

The same pattern of state-formation by invaders from outside is to be seen in a much more complete form in Dagomba, and presumably also in Mamprussi, though there the evidence is less well defined. Here the process of symbiosis is more complete, but it is interesting to note that it has gone further in western Dagomba, the region first settled by the invaders from the northeast, than it has in eastern Dagomba, an area of later expansion. In western Dagomba, the invaders have totally eclipsed the original Gur kinship groups: the traditions, which are totally those of the invaders, refer significantly to the killing of the *tengdanas*, the priest-leaders of the original holders of the soil, and to marrying into their families. In eastern Dagomba, incorporated into the state only after the rise of Gonja in the west in the seventeenth century had forced the Dagomba to move the centre of gravity of their state further to the east, more of the old social structure remains. Further east still, protected by the marshes of the Oti River from the cavalry of the state-forming invaders, among the Konkomba the primitive kinship form of society has survived almost intact, and it is more than a presumption that it was people like these Konkomba groups who provided the mass of the material that the Dagomba invaders fashioned into their state.[46]

From evidence already discussed, it would seem that the trade route towards the Gold Coast from the northwest, from Mande-land, developed earlier than that from the northeast, from Hausaland. This may afford at least a partial explanation for the fact that the first European to visit Mossi and Mamprussi, Capt. L. G. Binger, during his journey of 1889–90, saw in their states abundant features of Mande provenance.[47] Such features would seem less in evidence in Dagomba, the most southerly state of the Mossi-Mamprussi-Dagomba complex (which was not visited by Binger), but their common earliest traditions suggest that when the state-forming immigrants arrived from the northeast, there was already a Mande influence of some kind existent among the Gur groups, and that in Mossi certainly, and possibly in Mamprussi also, the process of social symbiosis covered Mande peoples as well as Gur-speaking autochthones.[48]

Be this as it may, the picture we get from Gonja and Dagomba is one of comparatively small groups of invaders forming the more numerous peoples of pre-existent kinship groups into states, and in course of time merging with them ethnically and linguistically. This process of the eventual mergence of small groups of state-forming conquerors with the more numerous populations of the conquered would seem to be the key to a great deal of African history.[49] It would seem almost certain that the Akan traditions of migration from the north or northwest are not necessarily the traditions of the bulk of the people, but more essentially those of successive waves of immigrants who organised earlier kinship groups into political states of the type being developed further north in the Sudan.

In the case of Gonja, we know that the earlier inhabitants were already what we should now call Akans; in the case of Dagomba, we can deduce that they were Konkomba or similar Gur-speaking groups. It is also known that when the Gã arrived from the east about the fifteenth century they infiltrated among and sometimes absorbed Akan groups, the Kpesi and the Afutu. Remnant groups of these peoples still survive to the immediate west of the Gã area; their languages or dialects are closely related to the Guang of Gonja. Similar languages are found in pockets north of the Gã and through the Volta gap in the Akwapim-Togo hills back towards Gonja. It has been inferred from this linguistic evidence that the first Akan migrations to reach the coast came from the north through the Volta gap in a clockwise sweep around the borders of the forest, and that the Akan penetration directly through the forest towards the sea was a later phenomenon.[50] It may be that previously the forest was but thinly occupied, and that its settlement by the Akans does represent more of a movement en masse. However, the evidence of the Gonja and Gã migrations suggests that the first Akan settlements were appreciably earlier; with the result that, even if the Akan state-formers had not tended to eclipse earlier traditions (as has undoubtedly been the case),[51] the formation of the first Akan states took place at too remote a period of time for us to have any idea of what the pre-state peoples were like.

In general terms, however, just as we can consider the early history of Dagomba, Mamprussi, and Gonja essentially as the impingement into a mass of indigenous Gur- or Kwa-speaking peoples, of state-forming invaders coming down the lines of the major northeastern and northwestern trade routes which linked the Gold Coast to the great empires and commercial centres of the Sudan, so too it is permissible to think of the creators of the Akan states impinging along the northwestern highway into an already existent pattern of "Kwa" kinship groups distributed along their east-west coastwise axis. This leads us to take another look at the westwards movement along this axis from what is now southwestern Nigeria, in particular from the land of the Yoruba states and of Benin, of the Gã and Ewe Kwa-speaking peoples. It has already been remarked that much of the political organisation of these peoples is Akan-inspired, that is, that it derives indirectly from the northwestern impulse from the Sudan of state formation. On the other hand, in point of time the Gã and Ewe movements would seem to be associated, as an end product, with successive waves of state-forming movements coming south or southwestwards from the Sudan east of the Gold Coast, in what is now Nigeria. These are the "Kisra," "Oduduwa," and "Bayajidda" invasions remembered in the traditions of the peoples of Hausaland, Nupe, Yorubaland, and Benin. The circumstances suggest that the effects of these invasions were deflected westwards by the coast, but that the state-forming impulse itself

did not proceed much further west than Ketu, or, at a second re-
move, to what became Dahomey. Recent work by Dr. Biobaku
suggests that while the ancestors of the Gã and Ewe might derive
from the earliest remembered invasion of Yorubaland from the
north, the "Kisra" invasion, their westwards emigration could be
a flight from the later consequences of the second major state-
forming movement, the "Oduduwa" invasion, which produced
great states like Oyo and Benin which expanded by conquest.[52]

The general Gold Coast pattern might therefore be tentatively
viewed in something like the following terms. Before about the
eleventh century, the land was occupied by a number of small
kinship groups. Those in the northern savanna we may call "Gur"
groups; those in the south, in or near the forest, we may call
"Kwa" groups. In remote and isolated parts of the country, such
as the Oti marshes and some mountain regions of Togoland, kinship groups of these types still survive in something like their
original form; the process of state-formation has not taken place
at all. Elsewhere, however, this primitive pattern has been upset
by the state-forming activities of relatively small groups of im-
migrant Negroes coming southwards as a consequence of the
process of change initiated in the Sudan through the expansion
of the Mediterranean peoples and their trade. The immigrants
tended to approach the Gold Coast either along the northwestern
trade route, from the region in which Ghana, Mali, and other
great predominantly Mande states emerged, or along the northeastern trade route from the region of Hausaland and Bornu. The
newcomers began to create states on the Sudanese model from
among the local kinship groups on which they imposed themselves, and with whose members they eventually merged in race
and language.

From the northeast came the founding ancestors of Dagomba
and Mamprussi, arriving about the fifteenth century. At about
the same time the Gã and Ewe began to arrive from the east,
possibly as a consequence of state-forming upheavals in what is
now southwestern Nigeria. A number of waves arrived from the
northwest, the earliest settling just north of the forest by about
the thirteenth century, and then spreading eastwards round it

through the Volta gap to the sea and then westwards along the coast. These early waves produced, among others, the first Akan groups of what is now Gonja and of the coastlands, and large or important states such as Bono and Banda. Later waves tended to push into and through the forest, creating there and at the coast a large number of small states, small perhaps because the difficulty of movement in and through the forest tended to break the immigrants up into small groups. The Fante states of the coast emerged from this movement, while many of the small forest states were eventually, in the eighteenth century, incorporated into the Ashanti Union. Finally, about the seventeenth century, the creators of modern Gonja appeared, who, by the time of the arrival of the Europeans at the end of the nineteenth century, had hardly succeeded in forming the earlier Akan groups into a coherent state.

CHAPTER II

European Contacts and Influences

The developments in the western Sahara and the western Sudan considered in the previous chapter—namely the North African conquest of the desert, the establishment of caravan routes linking North Africa with the Negro peoples of the western Sudan, and the development there of considerable political states—could by no means pass unnoticed in the countries of southwestern Europe on the northern shore of the Mediterranean. Indeed, a case can be made out for considering these developments to be an extension of what might be termed Mediterranean history.

There are two basic and interlinked explanations for southwestern Europe's awareness of and interest in the course of events in northwestern Africa. The first is, of course, the expansion of Islam, the agents of which in southwestern Europe were as much

31

North African Berbers as Arabs from the orient. Early in the eighth century the greater part of the Iberian peninsula was subjugated by Muslims from North Africa, who for a time even penetrated into southern France, and Sicily and the other islands of the western Mediterranean also came under Muslim dominion. For several centuries, peoples whom we would today think of as Europeans, but who should then be regarded rather as the northern inhabitants of a Mediterranean world—the world of the Phoenicians, the Greeks, and the Romans, for whom the Mediterranean had been a centre, not a frontier—lived within the sphere of Muslim culture and civilisation, and as a result gained much that was immediately denied to more northerly Europeans. For at this time, the Muslim world, drawing on the resources of Hellenistic, Aramaic, and Indo-Persian cultures and synthesizing them all through its great contribution of the Arabic language, was incomparably rich in intellectual culture, in philosophy, natural science, medicine, geography, and other fields. The city of Cordoba in Andalusia, it should be remembered, was a centre of Islamic learning and scholarship second only to Baghdad. Here in the eleventh century, lived Al Bakri, one of the greatest early authorities for the geography of northern Africa, to whom we owe the only detailed written description of ancient Ghana at the peak of its power.[1] Idrisi, perhaps the greatest of Islamic geographers, worked in Sicily.[2] Ibn Khaldun, the author of a monumental history of the Berbers, a man who may well be thought to have a better claim than Herodotus to be considered the father of history, at least as a critical study, came of a Berber family which settled in Spain in the ninth century, and though himself a native of Tunis, spent an appreciable portion of his active career in the Iberian peninsula.[3] Leo Africanus, a native of Spain, and the last of the great Islamic authorities on the Sudan, seems to have been equally at home on both the Christian and the Muslim shores of the Mediterranean.[4] Admittedly the advent of the Normans and the rise of Christian nationalisms in the Iberian peninsula eventually limited the frontiers of Islam to the southern shores of the Mediterranean, but the process was not complete until as late as 1492, and the conquerors were inevitably heirs to many of the traditions of Islamic civilisation. In particular, they had available to them the fund of Arabic knowledge about the geography of the Sudan and the history of its peoples.[5]

Southern European *awareness* of the Sudan thus evolved more or less naturally out of the fact that the Mediterranean had not served as a barrier to the expansion of Islam, less of a barrier perhaps even than the Sahara. Southern European *interest* in the Sudan, in Negro Africa, evolved more particularly through commercial contacts with North Africa. Italian merchants seem to have begun to visit the ports of the Maghrib as early as the ninth century. By the twelfth and thirteenth centuries, we find communities of merchants from the leading north Italian trading city-states, and also from Sicily and southern Italy, Marseilles, and Catalonia, established on shore at the major North African ports, and evidently engaged in thriving trade. The overt hostility between Christianity and Islam during the period of the Crusades tended to bring the merchants and seamen of the ports and trading states of Italy, Provence, and Catalonia into even closer contact with their opposite numbers in North Africa. Indeed, the merchant seafarers of southwestern Europe turned the businesses of transporting crusading armies and ransoming Christian captives to good commercial account, and the period of hostilities, in fact, afforded new and greater opportunities for both Christian and Muslim merchants to enlarge their capital and to work out new methods for its employment to the benefit of themselves and their mutual relations.[6]

European trade with the ports of North Africa naturally linked up with trades further afield under Muslim control. Thus trade with Egypt, and with ports in the Levant, Asia Minor, and the Black Sea, afforded Europe access to the luxury exports of Asia. In a similar way, trade with the ports of North Africa naturally linked up with the trans-Saharan trade conducted by North African merchants. In general terms, the form of the trade was an exchange of European manufactures, particularly metalware, for foodstuffs and raw materials. Although much of the latter—for example cereals, dried fruits, olives, and so forth—originated in

North Africa, some of the North African exports derived ultimately from the Sahara and the Sudan—for example gold, salt, slaves, and leather—and equally some of the manufactures traded by North African merchants in the Sudan—for example glass beads and metalware—had come originally from southern Europe.

But although in this way southern Europe was trading indirectly with the Sudan, the merchants and rulers of North Africa took good care to bar direct European access to the trans-Saharan trade routes. There were isolated instances of Europeans penetrating along these routes and even returning to tell the tale—perhaps the best-known cases are those of the Genoese merchant Antonio Malfante, who visited Touat in 1447, and of the Toulousian, Anselme d'Isalguier, who is reputed to have lived as far afield as Gao on the Niger during 1405–13.[7] But the point is that these were isolated instances; the North Africans would in no sense tolerate any concerted attempt by Europeans to gain entry into their own particular commercial empire.

But the reports of men like Malfante and Isalguier, and still more of men like the Polos or John of Montecorvino who had seen the infinitely greater riches of the trade of eastern Asia, were bound to stimulate attempts to establish direct European access to the world beyond Islam, to the Negro land of gold, and even, if possible, to the sophisticated wealth of the Indies and China. Even if medieval Europeans were unaware of the ancient attempts at the circumnavigation of Africa, one of which, the voyage from east to west by Phoenician sailors under the orders of King Necco of Egypt about 600 B.C., seems likely to have been successful,[8] contact with the Arab geographers, with their notion of *al-Bahr al-Muhit,* "the all-encircling sea," and their detailed knowledge of the geography of the Sudan and of the East African coast, was bound eventually to suggest the idea that it would be *theoretically* possible to reach West Africa, and even to gain access to the Indian Ocean, by sea. The principal issue would be to determine whether such voyages were *practicable* for the ships and navigators of the time.

The earliest known post-classical attempt to circumnavigate

Africa and to reach the Indies via the Atlantic was that of the Vivaldi brothers, who left Genoa in 1291 with a well-equipped expedition and sailed out through the Straits of Gibraltar. No certain news of the fate of their enterprise ever returned to Europe,[9] thus in effect proving, what was undoubtedly the case, that Mediterranean galleys were not suitable vehicles for long ocean voyages. However, at this time the Iberian communities fronting the Atlantic were evolving tough little sailing vessels, leading to the caravel type, which were to make the conquest of the oceans a practical proposition. The first use of these ships was for fishing and trade in European waters; the technical skills of navigation and cartography which were required for long voyages of exploration were lacking. But these the Italians could and did provide. Thus in 1284, the Genoese Benedetto Zaccaria was recruited as admiral of Castile (and later became admiral of France); in 1317, Manuel Pezagno was invited from Genoa by King Diniz of Portugal to organise the Portuguese navy; in the 1330's and 1340's, we find Genoese sailors joining with Portuguese in the exploration of the Canary Islands, although it was Normans and Castilians who later embarked on their exploitation. Leadership in the making of the earliest scientific maritime charts, the *portolani,* passed in the fourteenth century from northern Italy to Majorca, and with it went a remarkably accurate and detailed knowledge of the geography of the western Sudan, as is revealed, for instance, in the Catalan Atlas attributed to Abraham Cresques (*c.* 1375). In the following century, primacy in cartography, and in navigational knowledge generally, moved even further west, to Portugal.[10] Even in the fifteenth and early sixteenth centuries, there remains a noticeably Italianate flavour in Iberian maritime expansion. Contemporary Portuguese and Castilian accounts naturally stress the national nature of their momentous oversea enterprises, but even so names like Cadamosto and Usodimare (from Venice), Columbus (from Genoa), and Vespucci (from Florence) remain as a permanent witness to the share in them of Italian skill and capital.

This migration of navigational and cartographical expertise westwards from the Italian city-states to the shores of the Atlantic was natural enough in the circumstances of the time. The old Mediterranean trade with the orient was becoming more and more engrossed by Venice, so that the seamen, merchants, and bankers of the other Italian trading cities, such as Genoa, were ready to grasp new opportunities outside the Mediterranean. The new states of western Europe, whose sailors and merchants were conquering the ocean and developing new bulk trades, and whose rulers were naturally eager to increase their wealth and power, provided just the opportunities the Italians looked for.

Nowhere more was this the case than in the Iberian peninsula, whose Christian princes were engaged in an all-out struggle to evict Islam and the Moors from their soil. In the process they evolved new national states with highly centralised and powerful systems of Christian government. As the Moors were expelled, it was natural that these states should seek to extend their campaigns across the Mediterranean into Morocco, if only to prevent a recrudescence of Moorish power and to oppose the maritime counterattacks which were the basis of corsairing. Thus the Iberian nations and their rulers came into even closer contact with the people of North Africa and with their trade with the Sudan, and so, too, they became more intimately concerned with any scheme which might present itself for achieving direct relations with lands on the further side of the Muslim world, to the south and east, desiring perhaps to find in them new allies for the crusade against Islam, and certainly interested in diverting the trade of such lands from the Muslims to themselves. In this connection, both the Iberian princes and their Italian merchant allies were bound to pay particular attention to West Africa as a source of gold. This was not only because gold was intrinsically desirable to them both, but also because it was an essential article in European trade with the orient, since, from Roman times at least,[11] European goods were less in demand in Asia than Asian produce was in Europe, and the balance had to be made up by European exports of bullion and specie.

In the long run, the strongest and most highly centralised of the new Atlantic states that emerged from the struggle with the Moors in the Iberian peninsula was Castile. But the power and centralisation of the Castilian monarchy were in part a reflection of the fact that it was Castile which was longest preoccupied with the conflict with the Moors on the soil of the peninsula itself. Whereas Granada did not fall to the Christians of Castile until 1492, Portugal had finally freed herself from the Moorish occupation by the reconquest of the Algarve, completed as early as 1250. Thus the Portuguese gained freedom for the development of the arts of peace and for the emergence of a commercial bourgeoisie. With the advent of the house of Aviz in 1383–85 as the champions of popular rights against the pretensions of the nobility, the clergy, and the rulers of Castile, the political, economic, and seafaring interests of Portugal were at once ripe for expansion, and it was Portugal, not Castile, that led the way in North African conquests and in the planned exploration and exploitation of the coasts of West Africa.[12]

The key figure in the early stages of this expansion was Henry the Navigator, the third son of King John I, the founder of the Aviz dynasty. The whole of Henry's active career is bound up with Africa. It opened in 1415 when, as a young man of twenty-one, he took a leading part in the capture of Ceuta from the Moors, an action which he and his brothers had urged on King John with the enthusiastic support of the mercantile class, and for which he was rewarded with the governorship of the town, the first part of the African continent to come under Portuguese rule. When he died in 1460, he had just returned from an unsuccessful expedition against Tangier. Much of Henry's working life was in fact taken up with the Portuguese attempt to conquer Morocco, or at least to control its coastline, an attempt which was not finally abandoned until after the disaster of Al-Ksar al-Kabir (Alcazar Quivir) in 1578. But it is not for his close association with the Portuguese in Morocco that Henry is to be remembered. His great achievement was that, in association with his brother Dom Pedro, King John's second son, he directed the systematic exploration of the West African coastline beyond Cape Bojador, the Saharan headland just south of the Canary Islands which had hitherto been the accepted southern limit of European navigation.

The Portuguese were by no means the only Europeans engaged in enterprises of West African exploration during the fifteenth century. Ships from the neighbouring Atlantic ports of Castile seem never to have been far behind those of Lagos and Lisbon in West African ventures, at least until Columbus's discoveries opened up new and exclusively Castilian opportunities for overseas adventure and profit.[13] But Portuguese primacy in West African exploration and trade was ensured through the fact that their voyages were not the haphazard ventures of individual merchants and seamen, but part of a grand, methodical, planned scheme of national expansion directed by a member of the royal house. Henry established himself at Sagres, close by Cape St. Vincent, the southwestern extremity of Portugal, and there surrounded himself with the best astronomers, geographers, cartographers he could secure.[14] As his captains probed methodically down the African coastline, their experiences and observations were reported back to Sagres to be sifted and collated and combined with the best available geographical and maritime knowledge of Europe and Islam, so that each new explorer could be better instructed and equipped than the last.[15]

The aims of Henry's enterprise were officially stated during his lifetime by the court chronicler, Azurara. He does appear to have had a genuine interest in extending the limits of geographical knowledge, but he sought to do so more particularly because he wished to extend the Portuguese campaign against the Muslims of North Africa by passing beyond the limits of Islamic power and making contact with non-Muslim peoples whose trade, and possibly power, would strengthen Portugal in her national crusade, and who would provide converts for the expansion of Christendom.[16] The boundaries of Henry's ambitions are still a matter for discussion. It seems practically certain that he expected to link up with the Christian kingdom of Abyssinia, which in his lifetime was beginning to emerge out of the mists of the Prester John legend. It is nowadays commonly supposed that his ultimate goal was to gain direct access to the Indies and to the Asian trade so much valued in Europe. Henry and his advisers undoubtedly believed that there was no fundamental geographical barrier which would make the circumnavigation of Africa impossible, but what they could not know, and what they were determined to find out, was whether it was a practicable proposition with the equipment at their disposal. The very size of the African continent was unknown,[17] and the practicability of establishing regular ocean communication with the shores of the Indian Ocean could only be ascertained by painstaking processes of exploration, experiment, and reflection, the cost of which in time, effort, and money could not be foreseen and might prove prohibitive. But in the meantime there was another, closer prize which would help to support the larger plan until it could pay its own way. The Portuguese were well informed about the trans-Saharan gold trade, and knew that the gold came from lands beyond the effective limits of Muslim power, from the Negroland of the Sudan. If they could pass the southern boundary of Islam in West Africa, they should be able to divert this gold, and the power that it brought, to their own ends.

The initial progress of Henry's explorers was slow, less perhaps because of the actual difficulties of navigation than of the psychological difficulties involved in venturing into the unknown, and because the Portuguese seamen at first found little to attract them further.[18] They were, of course, skirting the desolate western edge of the Sahara desert. But at length in 1445, they came to the mouth of the Senegal and to Cape Verde, and so to the northwestern corner of the land in Negro occupation, the land which the Portuguese called Guinea.

The significance of this achievement has tended to be obscured by argument as to the derivation of this name, Guinea. It seems first to have appeared in Europe's corpus of geographical knowledge in the form "Gunuia" in a Genoese map of *c.* 1320. Later variants include "Ginyia" (in the Catalan Atlas of 1375), "Ghinea," and "Gheneoa" (Leo Africanus, 1550). It has been suggested that the name is a corruption either of Ghana, or of Jenne (Djenne), one of the successors to Ghana among the commercial emporia of the western Sudan. A derivation from Ghana would seem to be unlikely if only on the ground that the pronunciation of the initial letter of Ghana, which is the Arabic *ghain,*

is more nearly "rh" than "gh." The derivation from Jenne, which
is accepted by some modern authorities, including Bovill,[19]
would seem to originate in Leo Africanus, whose text confuses
the town of Jenne with a "kingdom" of Gheneoa. But Leo also
says that the latter name is one used by merchants in the African
trade, and his most recent editors comment on this as follows:
"Kenawa, Gnawa, nom toujours en usage au Maroc pour désigner
les Noirs et leur pays." [20] Delafosse long ago pointed out that
the Moroccan Berber equivalent of the Arabic phrase *Bilad-as-
Sudan,* "the land of the black men," was *Akal-n-Iguinawen,* and
that as early as *c.* 1137 the Arabic geographer Al Zuhri had used
the name *Guinawa* for the westernmost zone of the Sudan.[21]

Surely then, our Guinea derives from the Moroccan term for
Negroland, or from the singular form *Aguinaw* or *Gnawa* meaning "black," and nothing is more natural than that the Portuguese, making their first contacts with Africa in Morocco, should
use the Moroccan name for the country which they first reached
in 1445. The matter is really placed beyond dispute by the words
used by Azurara, writing *c.* 1450, when he describes the discovery: "The inhabitants of this green land are all black; and for this
reason the land is called the land of the Negroes or land of
Guinea, and the men and women who inhabit it are called
Guineus, which is to say, blacks." [22]

This one sentence encompasses a great achievement. The
Portuguese explorers had finished with the Sahara and its desolate white sands. South of Cape Blanco, "the white cape," on
their maps they could now inscribe Cape Verde, "the green
cape," the symbol of fertility, the beginning of productive lands
where trade would be profitable. And these lands were beyond
the sphere of Muslim control; they were the lands of Negro
Africa whence came the gold which they and the Muslim merchants both coveted. They had achieved the first goal of their
ambitious enterprise.

The pace of this enterprise now began sensibly to quicken. By
the time of Henry's death in 1460, the Portuguese had explored
and were trading as far afield as Sierra Leone. Thereafter royal
sponsorship of the West African enterprise seems to have lagged

for a space. But it was hardly needed; the appetites of Portuguese merchants had been thoroughly whetted, and the Cape Verde Islands were being colonised as permanent bases for the African trade. In 1469, a Lisbon merchant, Fernão Gomes, entered into a contract with the Crown whereby for five years he secured a monopoly of the Guinea trade, save that reserved to the Cape Verde islanders by an earlier grant, in return for an annual rental and the condition that each year his captains should explore a further hundred leagues [23] of coastline. Two years later, early in 1471, two of Gomes's agents, João de Santarem and Pero de Escobar, reached a part of the coast where gold was so abundant that it quickly became known as *A Mina*, "the mine." [24] Europe had discovered the Gold Coast.[25]

Ever since Cape Bojador had been doubled in 1434, the Portuguese had kept a keen eye open for signs of the wealth in gold which their acquaintance with the trade of North Africa and with the Arabic authorities had led them to associate with the region they were exploring. Thus as early as 1441, an arm of the sea between Cape Bojador and Cape Blanco had received the name of Rio do Ouro because it was there that the Portuguese explorers had first secured a little gold. Somewhat larger quantities could be obtained by trade on the coasts around Cape Verde and southwards to about as far as Sierra Leone. This gold, as was remarked by Azurara in the case of Rio do Ouro,[26] originated from Wangara, and the amount secured by the Portuguese probably represented only an insignificant overflow from the main output, which continued to flow northwards by the established Muslim land routes. Try as they could, the Portuguese never succeeded in diverting any appreciable part of this flow into their own hands, principally because both the gold fields and the trade routes were too remote from the centres of their power on the coast.[27]

But Gomes's captains found that between the mouths of the Tano and Volta rivers there were numerous small states which showed abundant signs of wealth in gold, which was—and is—a common metal for purposes of personal and ritual decoration on the Gold Coast, especially among the chiefly classes; and they

found, too, that the people of these states were willing to exchange gold, more especially gold dust, for cloth, beads and
trinkets, and implements of baser metals such as iron, copper,
and brass, relatively rarer and more useful, and thus soon imported into the country in raw form as well. The Portuguese
supposed that somewhere in the interior, not very far from the
coast, there must be a gold mine of unparalleled fecundity, hence
of course the name Mina, which must already have been in use
by 1474 when King Afonso V granted Gomes the use of the sur-
name "da Mina." [28] In fact, the gold of Mina came from innumerable alluvial washings and small pits, rarely exceeding about
thirty feet in depth, scattered throughout a large part of the
forest behind the coast.[29] There seems no reason to doubt that
gold from the Gold Coast had been travelling northwards to the
Sudan and thence to North Africa. The Bono tradition which
bears on this subject has already been mentioned,[30] and it would
also seem significant that the Portuguese found that some of the
kinds of cloth that sold best on the Gold Coast were of Moroccan
manufacture.[31] But the trade to the north seems to have been
opened up only about the middle of the fourteenth century, little
more than a hundred years before the Portuguese discovery, and
the gold-bearing lands lay in the forest well to the south of the
effective limits of power of the Sudanese empires and their traders.
The Portuguese, therefore, had little difficulty in establishing
themselves as successful competitors with the northern traders.
Their line of communication was effectively shorter and more
efficient. One may indeed suppose that the Portuguese traders
began to siphon off more gold from the Gold Coast than was able
to reach North Africa by the long and indirect overland trade.

The discovery of such a source of wealth determined the
Portuguese Crown to resume direct control of the trade with
Guinea. Gomes's contract, which had been extended into a sixth
year, was not further renewed, and in 1474 King Afonso placed
the Guinea trade under the direction of his heir, Prince John.
Thereafter the progress of Portuguese maritime expansion was
rapid and spectacular. Within fourteen years, Bartholemeu Dias
had found the way into the Indian Ocean; in twenty-four, Vasco

da Gama had begun direct trade with India. This further exploration, and the development of Portuguese interests in the Congo, in eastern Africa, in India and the further East, do not concern us here. But the increasingly rapid pace of the advance following the discovery of the Gold Coast makes it hard to resist the conclusion that it was this discovery that provided the incentive for renewed royal interest and participation in Portuguese overseas expansion, and, indeed, provided the source of capital to enable it to be brought so swiftly to so triumphant a conclusion. By the early years of the sixteenth century, the Portuguese were in possession in West Africa, primarily in the Gold Coast, of a supply of gold which may possibly have accounted for one-tenth of the world's whole known gold supply at the time,[32] and this must have been a factor of some importance for the conduct of their trade in India and the East.

John II, who had succeeded to the throne in 1481, took early steps to ensure that this new supply of wealth should be under the exclusive control of the Portuguese, and of the Portuguese Crown in particular. As the contemporary chronicler, Ruy de Pina,[33] puts it, "The King, considering, as a wise man, the great profit and good health, which his subjects would receive in body and soul, and also how his merchandise, and the affairs of his honour, estate and service would be properly secured, if he were to possess in those parts of Mina a fortress of his own," [34] in 1481 despatched a trusted knight of his household, Diego da Azambuja, with instructions to erect such a fortress on the most suitable site which could be found on the central section of the Gold Coast.

Thus early in 1482, Da Azambuja and a selected and well-equipped party of sailors, soldiers, and artisans commenced the construction of the great castle of São Jorge da Mina, still the most impressive architectural monument on the Gold Coast, on a rocky little peninsula adjacent to the African settlement of Edina (now called Elmina). This settlement was known to the Portuguese as "the village of two parts," since the little river Benya, which skirts the northeastern walls of the castle, formed the boundary between the two states of Edina and Fetu, and there was a Fetu settlement on its eastern bank. In subsequent years, the Portuguese supplemented Elmina with other fortresses, at Axim and Shama (where the Portuguese had first landed in 1471) on the coast to the west, and at Accra to the east. Unlike the other three forts, which have survived intact to this day, no vestiges of this last fort are now to be seen. According to De Marees (1602), it was destroyed by the Gã in 1576.[35] It is possible that the English Fort James, erected in the seventeenth century, occupies its site.[36]

The purpose of these forts, which between them covered the whole length of the coastline from which gold could be obtained, was to ensure that the maritime trade of the Gold Coast remained under the exclusive control of the Portuguese Crown, safe from inroads by private Portuguese traders or by merchants from other seafaring nations of western Europe, from Castile, Flanders, France, and England in particular, who were naturally drawn to the West African trade by the success of the Portuguese. Although the crown's interests tended to suffer increasingly at the hands of incompetent and sometimes venal local officers in Africa, throughout the sixteenth century no other European power was strong enough to mount more than a fleeting challenge to the Portuguese position on the Gold Coast.

The beginning of the end of the Portuguese claim to a monopoly of the maritime trade of the Gold Coast was seen in 1598, when merchants from the Netherlands, then in revolt against their Spanish rulers, who since 1580 had been kings of Portugal also, succeeded in establishing the first permanent European trading footholds on the coast to rival those of the Portuguese. But Dutch interest in West African trade was relatively slight until in 1637, Prince Maurice of Nassau, engaged on behalf of the Dutch West India Company in the conquest of Portuguese Brazil, realized that the prosperity of the Company's new American empire rested in the last resort on an assured supply of slave labour from West Africa, and accordingly embarked on an energetic campaign to capture the Portuguese trading bases in West Africa.[37] By 1642, the last of the Portuguese forts on the Gold Coast had fallen to the Dutch Company, and thereafter, although from time to time the Portuguese traded on the Gold Coast, they never again held any permanent bases on its shores.

The Portuguese had begun to trade in Negro slaves as early as the 1440's, transporting them first in comparatively small numbers for work on the agricultural lands redeemed from the Moors in the Iberian peninsula, and then, from about 1513 onwards, in increasingly greater numbers to provide a labour force for the plantations and mines of the new empire which the Spaniards were establishing at the expense of the indigenous population of the Caribbean islands and the adjacent American mainland. The Portuguese themselves had a requirement for slave labour in the plantation production of tropical crops, particularly sugar, first in their Atlantic islands, Madeira, the Azores, and the Cape Verde archipelago, which, with the Spanish Canaries, were the nursery ground from which the seeds of the plantation system—and much else besides—were transplanted to America; then in the islands of the Gulf of Guinea, such as Fernando Po and São Thomé, where the culture of the sugar cane by Portuguese colonists became established during the first twenty years of the sixteenth century; [38] and ultimately in Brazil, on the coastal lowlands of which a Portuguese plantation economy began to develop with increasing success and prosperity after about the middle of the sixteenth century. [39] It was to enable this economy to continue for the benefit of the Dutch conquerors of Northern Brazil that Maurice of Nassau undertook the conquest of the Portuguese trading stations on the coast of West Africa.

However, it would not seem that the Portuguese ever looked particularly to the Gold Coast for their supply of Negro slaves. Indeed there is evidence that at first, in the sixteenth century, the Portuguese were actually *importing* slaves into the Gold Coast from other parts of West Africa, particularly from Benin and the region of the Niger delta. [40] The main Portuguese sources of slaves seem to have lain further north, around the Senegal and the Gambia, and further south, around the Niger delta, and, increasingly, south of the Congo, in Angola, which was the most convenient source of supply for Brazil. Portuguese trading posts in

these regions were also captured by the Dutch during the years
1637–42, only to be retaken by the Portuguese during their remarkable national and colonial renaissance of the later 1640's and
the 1650's, when they also succeeded in finally expelling the
Dutch from Brazil.[41] However, these reverses by no means de-
terred the Dutch West India Company from the intention of
engaging in the large-scale exploitation of a trans-Atlantic slave
trade. The potentialities of the demand for slaves in the Spanish
colonies in America, and in the new English and French plantation colonies which were being set up in the Caribbean in the
wake of the Dutch destruction of Spanish naval power, were
enormous, and the supply of slaves to these markets was an important element in the achievement of a further goal, Dutch
domination of the carrying trade of all the European colonies in
America. But, of course, the Dutch could not for long maintain
this domination in the face of the new economic nationalisms
of post-revolutionary England and Colbertian France, and soon
English and French trading companies, with a greater or lesser
degree of state support, together with companies from other
states, notably Denmark, Sweden, and Brandenburg, where official or mercantile elements sought to emulate the Dutch example,
were entering into the lucrative business of competing with the
Dutch to supply the increasing demand for slaves from the vora-
cious and rapidly expanding plantation communities of the West
Indies and tropical America. The trans-Atlantic slave trade,
which in the sixteenth century had run at a mean level of perhaps
9,000 slaves a year, rapidly grew in volume, so that even conservative estimates put the total number of African slaves supplied
to America in the eighteenth century at something like 7,000,-
000, giving an annual mean of approximately eight times the
sixteenth-century figure.[42]

The effects of this great and competitive development of the
Atlantic slave trade on the Gold Coast and its peoples were far-
reaching. During the later part of the seventeenth century and
the early years of the eighteenth, English, Danish, and, for a brief
space, Swedish and Brandenburger, forts appeared on its shores
alongside those which the Dutch had captured from the Portu-

guese or had built for themselves. At first, during the period which is marked out in European history by the Anglo-Dutch wars and the wars of the Spanish and Austrian successions, these forts were apt to change hands quite frequently, but by the mid-eighteenth century a stable pattern had emerged which was to remain for something like a century. From Axim in the west to Accra in the east, Dutch and English forts were interspersed almost evenly at almost all the major coastal trading centres of the numerous small states of the Gold Coast littoral; from Accra eastwards to just beyond the Volta, developed a line of somewhat less pretentious Danish forts. Excluding subsidiary trading stations, or lodges, there were something like thirty major stone- or brick-built forts, garrisoned by Dutch, English, or Danish companies each of which held a legal monopoly of their country's slave trade, along something like 300 miles of coast, an average it will be seen of about one fort to every ten miles, a far higher concentration of European military architecture than anywhere else in Africa.[43]

Since in the Portuguese era, the Gold Coast apparently had no particular reputation as a source of supply for African slaves, what explanation is there for the great concentration there of competitive European effort during the heyday of the slave trade? A partial answer is provided by the continued attraction of the Gold Coast to European merchants as a source of gold. An estimate of the volume of this trade to Europeans made at the beginning of the eighteenth century suggests that in a good year it may have been worth as much as £200,000 sterling a year at contemporary values, nearly $2,000,000 at the present-day price of the metal, and it must be remembered, of course, that gold was a very much scarcer commodity then than now.[44] Nevertheless, the eighteenth-century forts were primarily maintained as depots in which slaves awaiting shipment and stocks of trade goods to be exchanged for slaves could be held; and east of Accra, along a coast to which the Danes extended the construction of forts (to as far as Keta) largely only after 1750, there was practically no gold to be obtained.

The prime reason for the concentration of slave-trading forts on the Gold Coast would seem to be that from the earlier trade, primarily in gold, the natives of the Gold Coast had developed a growing taste for European imports and had evolved a competent commercial organisation for dealing with these imports and distributing them in the hinterland. Despite the fact that there is no evidence to suggest that in the West African coastal and forest lands before the advent of Europeans, there had ever been any large-scale trade in slaves, such as undoubtedly developed in the West African Sudan following its opening-up to trade from North Africa, there were already slaves in coastal society, and such slaves already had what might be called a cash value. For example, it was possible for a man to "pawn," that is, pledge, a slave or a kinsman or even himself, as security for a debt. Thus when the emphasis of European trade in West Africa began to shift from gold and ivory and other inanimate commodities towards slaves, no great difficulty was occasioned among the African commercial communities in regarding slaves as commodities with a realisable value in terms of European manufactures. Moreover, if there were moral or economic limits to the extent to which any particular coastal community could denude itself of its own people by selling them into slavery to Europeans, there were appreciable numbers of less sophisticated peoples further in the interior who could be captured at little expense to the coastal communities other than the expenditure of a certain amount of powder and shot, which, together with the necessary firearms, were readily procurable from European traders. And so the European traders and the mercantile communities of the West African coastline joined together in an unholy partnership to provide profits for themselves out of the business of extracting human beings from Africa and selling them to provide a labour force for the plantations of the New World.

We are not so much concerned here with the slave trade as with its effects on West Africa and on the Gold Coast in particular. But two points about the trade should be made. First, that the Gold Coast contribution to it from about the middle of the seventeenth century to the end of the eighteenth, seems never to have been more than about ten thousand slaves a year.[45] At first the exports from the Gold Coast provided a considerable share of the total trade, but throughout the eighteenth century, as the total volume of the trade increased, the Gold Coast's proportion of it decreased. The additional slaves required for America were taken increasingly from the coasts to the east and south of the Gold Coast. The eastwards extension of Danish forts that has already been mentioned is symptomatic of this; [46] so, too, is the name Slave Coast which came to be applied to the coastline immediately to the east of the Gold Coast, though ultimately the centre of gravity of the slave trade moved even further away, to the Niger delta and beyond towards the Congo.

Secondly, we should note that both in the slave trade in general, and in trade on the Gold Coast in particular, the British had, by the end of the eighteenth century, secured a position of easy dominance, over half of the trade being in the hands of the merchants of this one nation.[47]

The relationship between the European merchants in their Gold Coast forts and the African coastal communities has just been described as a partnership, and a partnership implies the equality of the partners. In view of what happened to Africa in the nineteenth century, it may seem strange to refer to the eighteenth-century relationship between Europeans and Africans on the Gold Coast as one of equality, but it would seem that essentially this was what it was, though both the equality and the partnership were somewhat uneasy. The Gold Coast states did not want Europeans to build themselves fortified trading stations on their shores. Right at the beginning, D'Azambuja was only able to build his fort in the teeth of appreciable and active local hostility.[48] But if the construction of forts was the price which Africans had to pay for European trade, then it was a price which they were increasingly prepared to pay—on certain conditions. The principal one of these conditions came to be that there should be no formal infringement of the sovereignty of the states. As far back as the Portuguese period, the custom developed of the Europeans making regular payments to the local rulers. On the European side these payments may have originally been intended as subsidies to facilitate trade. However, in many cases arrangements regarding them became embodied in documents, called "Notes," held by the Gold Coast rulers, which could be interpreted as providing that the payments were rent for the land on which the forts had been built. [49]

Formally, therefore, the Europeans were subject to the law of the native states, and this was the case in practice if they wandered too far from their forts, or at least from the coast dominated by them. The purpose of the forts at the time when most of them were built, between c. 1650 and c. 1750, was primarily to protect their occupants and their trade from the attentions of their European rivals; but they did also, of course, serve to give their inhabitants a measure of immunity from the attentions of hostile Africans. However, this immunity was never complete. Sometimes the forts were better designed for seaward than for landward defence; their garrisons and supplies were seldom adequate to resist a prolonged siege from the land.[50] There are cases on record of African forces capturing forts, and holding them for periods of several years; there are many more cases of Europeans, including governors, receiving severe physical ill-treatment at the hands of the natives within sight of their forts.[51] If relations between European occupants of a particular fort and the people of the adjacent native state got thoroughly out of gear, then the latter could usually get their way by the simple device of withdrawing trade from the Europeans. Very often the threat alone would suffice; if an actual embargo were involved, the presence almost everywhere along the coast of rival European forts would almost certainly mean that it could be carried out without pecuniary loss to the Africans.

Nevertheless, there was a sense in which it may be said that European writs ran on the coast, at least as far as a gunshot would carry from the forts or ships of the European traders. The coastal trade attracted Africans to establish new urban settlements around the walls of the forts. The limits of these settlements took no account of the boundaries of the traditional native authorities. Their inhabitants included both permanent and transient emigrants from a number of states, some of them probably in the remote interior. The economically less successful of them were apt to make their living by performing services of various kinds for the occupants of the forts or even by finding regular employment as artisans, servants, or soldiers within them. The women of these new towns would, whether in or out of wedlock, provide wives for the Europeans and mothers for the families they begot while on the coast. The European language, customs, even religion, tended to become the only language, customs, and religion the community as a whole had in common.

There were indigenous ways in which the Africans could solve the divisions and conflicts of authority arising in such cosmopolitan communities, but in the last resort, particularly when it came to the defence of the community against outsiders, authority naturally tended to reside with the commander of the fort and its soldiers and guns, and the inhabitants would also naturally tend to side with their own particular group of Europeans in conflicts between the various European nationalities. Thus in a very real sense one begins to find references to Elmina as a Dutch town and Cape Coast as an English one, or even, in the case of Accra, where Dutch, English, and Danish forts were all in sight of one another, to Dutch, English, and Danish Accra respectively.[52]

In the broadest sense, what was happening to the Gold Coast, and to West Africa in general, was that it was being turned about-face. With the development of European maritime trade on the coast, new foci of economic and political change were evolving in the south, in the coastlands and in the adjacent forest country, instead of, as hitherto, in the northern savanna country bordering the Sahara with its camel-borne trade with North Africa. From the seventeenth century onwards the new foci began to eclipse the old in power and range, first because the new trade engendered by the traffic in slaves to America was bound, as a sea-borne trade, to outstrip in capacity the tenuous land routes across the desert; and then, during the later nineteenth and in the twentieth centuries, because the technological and ideological innovations brought to the West Africans from the new nations of Western Europe were vastly more potent than those introduced from the Muslim world, which, after about the fourteenth century, had entered upon a period of intellectual and scientific conservatism.

In *economic* terms, the effects of the about-face were felt pretty generally throughout West Africa, but nowhere were they stronger than in the Gold Coast, where European trade had long taken an unusually firm hold. In *political* terms, the change was perhaps most striking in the Gold Coast. In other regions where the slave trade was most firmly developed, for example on the Slave Coast or in the Niger delta, the same phenomena of a new concentration of population and of wealth close to the coast were equally in evidence. But in these areas the African authorities succeeded in avoiding, or at least in delaying, the onset of the political dangers implicit in the evolution of extra-tribal communities around centres of European power upon which they were increasingly dependent. This was in part because, as on the Slave Coast, the native rulers, learning from the experience of the adjacent Gold Coast, refused to allow the European traders to establish fortified and potentially extra-territorial posts; in part because the conditions in which the later slave trade was conducted by the Europeans did not seem to require the construction by them of permanent fortified depots.[53]

But on the Gold Coast, the plain fact that by the end of the eighteenth century the Europeans were potentially by far the strongest military power, began to involve them deeply in indigenous politics, far more deeply than men whose interest was essentially a commercial one ever desired to be involved. This was primarily a consequence of the emergence in the immediate hinterland of the Gold Coast of great states with an active policy of imperial aggrandisement.

The best known, and greatest, of these states is Ashanti, but in many ways it would seem that Ashanti only repeated, on a larger and more successful scale, the earlier example of Akwamu. Akwamu seems originally to have been a small state in the hinterland of Agona, west of Accra, but by the middle of the seventeenth century its centre of gravity had moved eastwards to the north of Accra. Then in 1677–81, Accra was conquered and its king and many of his people forced to flee to Little Popo.[54] Agona was conquered in 1688, and by 1702 the whole of the Accra plains to as far east as the Volta were subject to Akwamu. In this year the power of Akwamu was extended even further east, to as far as Whydah, which, until its conquest by Dahomey in 1727, became a tributary ally. At the peak of its power, we find Akwamu taking Christiansborg castle from the Danes and then selling it back to them,[55] and negotiating an alliance with the Dutch by which the latter recognized Akwamu sovereignty, agreed to render military assistance if Akwamu were attacked, and to pay to it a duty on the gold they bought.

This extensive empire was short-lived, for after a decisive defeat by Akim, to the west, in 1730, it disintegrated into its component parts, the modern Akan states of Akim Abuakwa and Akwapim, and the many small Gã and Adangme states. Evidently the rulers had not succeeded in establishing a sufficient community of interest among their subjects. This is hardly surprising because, although the initial movement to the east may have been occasioned by pressure from Akim, the subsequent development of the empire seems to have been dictated primarily by the desire of its rulers to engross the trade with the Europeans at the coast. Trade at Accra must have declined after the destruction of the Portuguese fort in 1576, but after *c.* 1633 it became of increasing importance, the Dutch, English, and Swedes [56] all establishing forts or lodges between 1642 and 1659. A likely explanation for this activity is the development of the Akim gold mines (Bosman, writing in 1700, said that the gold at Accra came from Akim, and that it was the richest and purest on the whole coast, which suggests that the mines might have been relatively young).[57] Consequently, we find Akwamu first extending parallel to the coast to control the routes inland from Accra, then occupying Accra, then the territory east of Accra, to close leaks in their trading monopoly, and finally occupying Agona, apparently to prevent Akim securing an independent outlet to the sea.[58]

If the beginnings of the Akwamu empire are to be sought in a reaction to the power of Akim, the origins of the great Ashanti Union are to be found, at the end of the seventeenth century, in the desire of a few small states in the central forest, many of whose rulers were of the same clan, to rid themselves of the attacks of the Doma in the west, and to assert their independence of the state of Denkyera, to which they were tributary. The architects of union were Osei Tutu, the King of Kumasi, and Okomfo Anokye, his chief priest. It is not insignificant that Osei Tutu spent part of his early life at the Akwamu court, to which he had fled following a misdemeanour committed when he was serving as a page to the King of Denkyera; that it was in Akwamu that he met Anokye; and that when he was called to the Kumasi stool, he returned with a retinue provided by the King of Akwamu. The political and military organisation of Ashanti was clearly influenced by that of Akwamu, although Osei Tutu and Okomfo Anokye were able to build on much surer foundations.

Okomfo Anokye's greatest achievement was the creation of the Golden Stool of Ashanti. Every Akan chief has his stool. It is equivalent to the throne of a European monarch, but after the death of its owner it is consecrated "and becomes the shrine for his spirit, which continues to guard his people." [59] Once the allied states had defeated Doma, Anokye determined that their alliance should be converted into a permanent union, strong enough to achieve lasting independence of Denkyera. This involved creating a common allegiance for the kings and peoples of the allied states which would transcend the allegiance which each owed to his own stool and those of his ancestors. Anokye's solution was to cause the Golden Stool to descend from the skies onto the knees of Osei Tutu in the sight of the allied rulers and their followers, and to get the latter to accept it as the repository of the spirit of the whole Ashanti people, and to swear allegiance to it and to the king of Kumasi as its custodian.

Thus a new nation was created which c. 1700 imposed a decisive defeat on Denkyera, and then proceeded to absorb other states which had been subject or allied to Denkyera. By the end of the eighteenth century, the Ashanti Union had become the dominant power in the forest west of Akim and north of the Fante states and had extended to a considerable distance north of the forest, incorporating Bono and Banda and imposing tribute on Gonja and Dagomba. Then in 1807, Ashanti embarked on the first of a series of invasions of the Fante and Gã coastal states.[60]

Although perhaps the evidence is less clear than it is in the case of Akwamu, or in the case of the comparable and contemporary expansion of Dahomey (whose point of departure bears much the same relation to the Slave Coast as does the Ashanti homeland to the Gold Coast), the fundamental explanation of the expansion of Ashanti, once the initial union had been consummated, must again be seen in terms of the desire for economic aggrandisement. The rise—and fall—of Akwamu took place sufficiently close to the coast to be within the range of European observation, while the rise of Dahomey was witnessed by Europeans actually resident in the country. No comparable first-hand written accounts of events within Ashanti are available until after 1817,[61] but the shape of Ashanti expansion once Denkyera had been defeated is such that we can be safe in supposing its underlying motives to have been essentially the same. Early expansion was first lateral and then northwards, the result being to secure a control of the supply of slaves and gold to the coastal markets, and of the distribution of the European imports received in exchange, over a wide area. Then, at the beginning of the nineteenth century, came the desire to eliminate the coastal middlemen and to determine the terms of trade directly with the Europeans on the coast.

The defeat of the small coastal states, whose own commercial rivalries and separate affiliations with the competing national groups of European traders made it difficult for them to unite for common defence, was not a difficut task for the experienced Ashanti armies. It had two far-reaching consequences: first, the passing into Ashanti hands by right of conquest of the "Notes" or leases for many of the coastal plots on which the European forts were built; [62] and secondly, a growing tendency for the peoples of the coastal states to look upon the Europeans as the only military powers strong enough to be able to stand up against Ashanti in their defence.

This was how matters stood on the Gold Coast in the years immediately after 1807, and it was just at this vital juncture in Gold Coast history that the home governments of the three European nations still possessed of forts on the coast each severally embarked on measures to outlaw participation in the slave trade for their subjects: Denmark in 1804, Britain in 1807, and the Netherlands in 1814. Since it was essentially the slave trade which had brought representatives of these nations to the Gold Coast, and made it worthwhile for them to continue there, with the political and social consequences for the coastal states that we have seen; and since it was the trade in slaves and gold which had occasioned the expansion of Ashanti, and so brought this new nation down to the coast; it is clear that the early years of the nineteenth century mark the beginning of an entirely new era in the history of the Gold Coast.

CHAPTER III

The Emergence
of Modern Ghana

The events of the early years of the nineteenth century which have just been discussed, namely, the abandonment by the Europeans trading to the Gold Coast of the traffic in slaves which had been the mainstay of their connection with West Africa and its peoples for nearly two hundred years, and the beginning of the Ashanti attempt to secure control of the coastal states with which the Europeans were trading, led to a confused situation in Gold Coast affairs which was not finally resolved until nearly a century later, until 1901, when the British finally took it upon themselves to accept full responsibility not only for the destinies of the Gold Coast proper, but also for Ashanti and its northern hinterland. It is possible, indeed, to view the whole of the nineteenth century in Gold Coast history as a period of transition in which the equal relations based on commerce, basically the slave trade, between the peoples of the coast and Europeans gradually gave way to a situation in which one particular European nation, Britain, achieved *political* dominion over an area very much more extensive than that involved in the earlier sphere of *commercial* contact.

The political history of the Gold Coast in the nineteenth century is complex, often indeed tortuous. Those who wish to study it in any detail can begin with Claridge's monumental *A History of the Gold Coast and Ashanti*, a work which, concentrating on political and diplomatic narrative, devotes nearly one thousand of its total of some twelve hundred pages to the affairs of this one century; or, more conveniently, with Mr. W. E. F. Ward's more modern and better balanced history.[1] Here we can do little more than to concentrate on one particular aspect of the nineteenth century and after, which would seem to have been of paramount importance in determining the shape of the new independent state of Ghana that eventually emerged from the colonial Gold Coast. This is the history of the constitutional relations between the British and the peoples of the coastal states, particularly of the Fante states of the central portion of the coast which were most directly affected by influences stemming from the British headquarters at Cape Coast Castle.

There are, however, other issues of nineteenth-century Gold Coast history which cannot be ignored, and which indeed would sometimes seem more vital and more urgent than the one singled out for attention here, and it is well that these issues be first briefly considered.

Issues of the Economic, Social, and Political Background

There was, to begin with, a quite fundamental economic question: if the export of slaves from the Gold Coast were to cease, what was there to take their place as a staple of the country's commercial ties with the outside world? Palm oil, gold, and rubber were each in turn thought to be the solution, but each in turn failed to come up to expectations. It was not until the early years of the twentieth century that the answer was finally found in the great success of the cocoa industry. But the problem was not in fact solely one of economics; it was bound up with a number of quite fundamental political issues.

If the later expansion of Ashanti is to be regarded fundamentally as an attempt to engross, or to control, the export of slaves and the profits to be gained from it, then a prerequisite for the cessation of the export of slaves from the Gold Coast was the prevention of the Ashanti hegemony over the coastal states which was threatened by the early nineteenth-century invasions. If a slave-trading Ashanti were to extend its control to the coast, then outlets for the export of slaves to the Americas would doubtless continue to be found. The British, Dutch, and Danish traders already possessed of footholds on the coast might be inhibited from purchasing slaves, but so long as a demand for slaves continued on the other side of the Atlantic—and it continued in effect into the 1880's [2]—there were bound to be merchants from some European or American nations willing, whether their country's laws allowed it or not, to supply this demand, and to do so in part by shipping slaves from the Gold Coast.

But what was to prevent an Ashanti hegemony over the coastlands? United action by the coastal states, perhaps. But then, as has been seen, the coastal states were severally small and weak, divided by jealousies reinforced by, or even originating in, commercial competition. Perhaps, too, the coastal states were already compromised. Their communities were themselves so much involved in the slave trade that for some of their members some degree of political dependence on Ashanti might seem a relatively small price to pay if in some measure the continuance of the slave trade and its profits could thereby be assured.

It was likely that the Ashanti advance could only be stemmed effectively by some kind of coöperation between the coastal peoples and the Europeans who already possessed the seeds of political power on the coast in the form of their forts and the influences radiating around them. But the Europeans had all themselves come to the Gold Coast for slaves. If the slave trade were now to be denied them, it was obviously an open question whether their traders would elect to remain on the coast; it was clearly far more questionable whether they would be willing to entertain new political responsibilities there. Such responsibilities would of necessity be expensive; whether or not they might ultimately lead to commercial benefits would equally necessarily be uncertain.

Furthermore, the British, the Dutch, and the Danes were themselves historically rivals on the Gold Coast. From their original and continuing commercial competition had now evolved competing spheres of political influence. One or more of them might well think their interests better served through some sort of coöperation with Ashanti rather than by making common cause with the coastal states to hold Ashanti at bay. Even if the representatives of one European power were not prepared to go as far as this in opposition to action taken by one of the others leading towards the development, under its influence, of a union of coastal states strong enough to stand against Ashanti, such action would be seriously inconvenienced, if not totally frustrated, without at least some degree of coöperation from the other European powers. It must not be forgotten that the Dutch and British forts were interspersed along the coast from Axim to Accra. There was not an exclusively Dutch and an exclusively British sphere of operations and influence; they were always in competition and usually to some degree overlapping. When in 1867 the Dutch and British eventually agreed to a treaty by which the Dutch were to take over the British forts west of Elmina in return for the British receiving the Dutch forts to the east of Cape Coast, the agreement broke down principally because the peoples of the states in which the forts were situated in many cases refused to concur in a change of traditional alliances that had been made without consulting them and their interests.[3] East of Accra, it is true, there was a stretch of the coast on which Danish forts and Danish influence were dominant, but it was not so remote that a contradictory or merely a different policy there would not cause complications for British or Dutch action. This difficulty became all the more acute as the sphere of European action began to move inland from essentially commercial affairs on the coast to embrace political matters in the hinterland.

In the long run, if one of the European nations chose to embark on a forward political policy in regard to the native states, it was likely to reach full consummation only in the event of the departure from the Gold Coast of its European rivals.

Not until 1872 was unequivocal European action against Ashanti really possible, with the result that for the best part of three-quarters of a century, the future of the coastal states remained uncertain, to the great detriment of their economic development. European merchants were naturally reluctant to venture their capital, and Africans were discouraged from developing new lines of trade to replace the traffic in slaves, in a country in which there were no settled relations between the coast and the hinterland.

A further, albeit perhaps lesser, difficulty was that as the European hold on the Gold Coast proper tended to increase, so the Ashanti drive towards the sea began to develop flanking movements to east and west. There is some evidence to show that these flanking movements, more particularly in the east, were in part at least intended to reopen the export of slaves by gaining access to coasts where European powers hostile to the slave trade were not so firmly established.[4] More seriously perhaps, they meant that trade with the Gold Coast hinterland tended to be diverted from the established coastal merchants, African as well as European, to traders on the adjacent Slave and Ivory Coasts. In this way, incidentally, Ashanti could secure the arms for her campaigns against the Gold Coast states which it was politic for the merchants there in business to deny her.[5]

As well as these fundamental economic and political problems, there also developed on the Gold Coast during the nineteenth century, a social issue of increasing perplexity and importance. The European reaction against the slave trade, in particular the British campaign against it, was by no means purely negative. The slave trade was regarded as a great crime which must be stopped, but it was not enough to try and ensure, principally through diplomatic and naval measures, that slaves were no longer taken from the shores of Africa for service in America. Positive action was needed in Africa itself. On the purely practical side, it soon became clear that in the Americas, diplomatic and naval action could never be wholly successful in preventing all potential trans-Atlantic slavers from gaining access to African shores.[6] Consequently, it became necessary somehow so to try to change conditions within Africa that slaves would not be presented for sale at its coastline. This practical aim was reinforced by the moral compulsion felt by many Europeans to offer to the peoples of Africa such positive principles as would lead to the ending of the slave trade, and of its attendant moral and material destruction, within the continent itself. Ultimately it was hoped to achieve the extinction of the very idea of slavery as an institution in Africa. The positive principles advocated varied widely both in degree and in kind. They extended from the simple preaching of Christianity and the Christian way of life, to the active development of agriculture and industry and the begetting of new and more profitable trades to swamp the slave trade, and even to the establishment of European administrations in Africa which would root out the slave trade, by force if need be, and impose totally new conceptions of government and behaviour upon its peoples.[7]

One of the earliest practical consequences of this new positive policy for Africa in the Gold Coast was the establishment there during the 1820's and 1830's of Christian missions, principally from Britain, Switzerland, and Germany. The consequences of mission activity were far-reaching, and indeed ultimately produced a climate of opinion in which many Africans became prepared to accept both the economic and the political implications of the positive campaign against the slave trade. Whether the missionaries wanted to or not—and most of them did not—they could not confine themselves solely to the preaching of a spiritual message. The effective propagation of Christianity in the Gold Coast, as elsewhere in Africa, involved them in the construction of new intellectual and material environments. It involved them in education in the broadest sense of the word, not only in the teaching of converts to read their Bibles in a European or a vernacular language, and in the training of African priests and ministers to continue and to expand the work of extending the knowledge and love of God to the people, but also in the establishing of new codes of conduct and the creating of a new physical environment, in which, for example, new standards of health, housing, and agriculture would help to conquer the destruction and uncertainty occasioned by tribal warfare, the slave trade, and simply by poverty.[8]

The establishment of the missions and their schools, in which Africans were taught not only to read and to write, but also to make better houses, farms, and tools, and were introduced to European, as opposed to African, concepts of thought and behaviour, intensified and greatly increased the pace of the social revolution which had already unconsciously been initiated by the European traders on the Gold Coast.[9] A new elite of European-trained and to some extent European-thinking merchants, ministers of religion, schoolteachers, lawyers, journalists, doctors, administrators, and politicians began to emerge in the coastal states during the second half of the nineteenth century, in part anxious to reform the traditional elites of African kinship society, in part competing with them for power.[10]

These economic, political, and social issues provide the essential background to the history of the Gold Coast in the nineteenth century, and it is important to realise the extent to which their resolution was an affair only of the last years of that century, or was even postponed into the twentieth century. Thus, although as early as 1821 the British decided to place their forts on the Gold Coast directly under the Colonial Office instead of leaving them in the hands of mercantile interests which did not seem to serve as a sufficiently positive agency for the suppression of slave-trading, subsequent British policy with regard to the Gold Coast, and the organisation and defence of the coastal states in relation to Ashanti, oscillated widely between negative and positive extremes. In 1828, the representation of British interests, and of the British interest, in the Gold Coast was again left to the traders; in 1843, the government began to return; in 1865, it declared its intention of withdrawing completely. In the 1830's and again in the later 1860's, we find the British considering the idea of attempting to solve the political problem by encouraging, or at least allowing, an inherently African-based political structure with no more than ideological stiffening from Europe.

On the European front, we find the Danes competing with the British for the establishment of spheres of political influence in the hinterland of Accra,[11] and the Dutch at least flirting with the idea of allying their interests with those of Ashanti.[12] The Danes, finding that their attempts to establish a profitable economic relation with the country to take the place of the slave trade were frustrated by the political uncertainties,[13] eventually ceded their forts to the British in 1850, but the field was not clear for exclusively British action until the final abandonment of the coast by the Dutch as late as 1872.

The implications of the Dutch departure were seen immediately in the British reversal of their 1865 policy of withdrawal and its corollary of permitting the coastal states to work out their own political salvation. A full-scale military invasion of Ashanti was mounted early in 1874, the first unequivocally positive British action towards Ashanti since the 1820's; and later in the same year the Gold Coast was declared to be a British colony. But these measures were neither of them decisive. A military defeat had been inflicted on Ashanti, but the territory was not incorporated in any stable political system, and indeed the Ashantis were left free to reconstruct their military union and all that it implied as a threat to the orderly and peaceful development of the coastlands. The proclamation of a British colony was indecisive because it had no defined geographical limits, and because the policy involved in such a step was almost indiscernible by the Africans in the light of the previous vacillation of British intentions, and in view of the British neglect to define any set relationship between the authority of their colonial administration and its jurisdiction and that of the native states.[14]

However, affairs were moving towards a climax. The establishment of some sort of colonial authority encouraged an ebullient influx of European capital in the expectation that the application of modern techniques of deep-level mining to the gold resources of the country would provide the firm base for European trade with the Gold Coast that had been lacking ever since the discontinuation of the slave trade. But the Gold Coast could not provide either the geological or the political conditions for the development of the second Witwatersrand that was at one time envisaged.[15] The gold-bearing strata were insufficiently rich and extensive; the African people too numerous and too tenacious of their economic and political rights. But gold mining, together with the need to secure firm hold of Ashanti, stimulated the government to embark on railway building, and the opening up of the forest by the railway and by motor roads made possible the development of what soon became far and away the Gold Coast's most important industry, the production for export, by the forest peoples working in their own way on their own lands, of cocoa for the world market. Here at last was the staple economic activity to provide funds for the economic and social development of the country, to provide indeed the essential foundations for political stability and ultimate independence. By the 1920's, the Gold Coast was providing half or more of the world's consumption of cocoa, and cocoa was constituting on an average two-thirds by value of the territory's exports.

In the meantime the advance of the French and German empires in West Africa had awakened the British government to an awareness of the vague and tenuous nature of its political footing on the Gold Coast. During the 1890's the British at last embarked on an active policy of extending their positive rule over the Gold Coast and its hinterland, a process which culminated in 1902 in three Orders in Council which constituted and defined the British Colonies of the Gold Coast and of Ashanti, and the British Protectorate of the Northern Territories, as they existed until 1957.[16] Thus at length was created a precise territorial frame around a number of African communities, all of whom were to be subjected to the levelling and leavening authority of the one European administration. This frame isolated a plane of reference on which two major forces could operate to bring modern Ghana to birth as an independent state. The point of departure for both these forces is to be found in the coastal states around the 1830's. One of them is the process of social change, originating principally in missionary activities, to which some reference has already been made; the other is the movement for political independence which arose initially out of the nature of the relations that began to be established during the 1830's between the British and the Fante states on the coast.

But before examining the latter in detail, it should first of all be remarked that the process of social change, although always cumulative in its effects, began to have significant results in the Gold Coast only after the major economic and political issues of the nineteenth century had been finally resolved. This of course was no accident, but it may particularly be ascribed to two developments: first, the emergence of the colonial government as a propagator of social change, ultimately by far the most powerful propagator; and, secondly, the increasing reinforcement of the process of social change by economic change caused essentially by the development of the cocoa industry.

From the time of Joseph Chamberlain's tenure of the Colonial Office in 1895–1903 onwards, the sphere of operation of British colonial administration tended increasingly to extend beyond its historic nineteenth-century role of maintaining law and order and administering justice, into the fields of economic development and social welfare. The latter covers many activities which have tended to accelerate the processes of social change in the Gold Coast and elsewhere, but none has been so far-reaching in its effects as government participation in the field of education. The first education ordinance of the Gold Coast government was in fact enacted as early as 1882,[17] only twelve years after the first British Education Act. Although for many years the Christian missions continued to provide the vast majority of the teachers and the schools for the expansion of a European-style education system in the Gold Coast, after 1882 the standards for such a system were set and an ever-increasing proportion of the cost of it was borne by government, with the result that the system developed both in depth and in width much more rapidly and completely than would otherwise have been feasible.[18]

Secondly, we must appreciate the extent to which the process of social change was accelerated and expanded by the new economic forces of the twentieth century. Before the great expansion of cocoa farming, outside the coastal towns in which dwelt the European traders and the African merchant classes, the country as a whole had hardly joined the world economy and, in a sense, dwelt outside the realm of a money economy altogether. The zone of production of palm kernels and oil, the nearest approach to a staple export in the nineteenth century after the ending of the slave trade, was a strip of land intermediate between the coast and the forest proper, and rarely further than about thirty miles inland. The principal gold-mining districts were also within about fifty miles from the coast and were concentrated in the extreme west. Towards the close of the nineteenth century, the export of wild rubber, which was a forest crop, began to be of importance, but the rubber trade was soon killed by overexploitation of the trees and by the competition of plantation-grown rubber from other areas.[19]

The last significant export of rubber from the Gold Coast was in 1912. In that year the country exported produce worth £3,-996,000 and imported goods to the value of £3,452,000, giving a total foreign trade of £7,448,000, or, since the population then numbered about 1,500,000, about £5 per inhabitant. In 1950, exports were worth £91,250,000 and imports £63,313,000, a total trade of some £154,663,000, or, with a population of some 4,112,000, nearly £38 per head.[20] This great change was almost entirely due to the development, throughout the forest zone, of the production of cocoa as a cash crop for export.

The cocoa tree was traditionally introduced into the Gold Coast from Fernando Po in 1879.[21] Cocoa proved a simple crop to grow under Gold Coast conditions. The soil and climate of the forest are just right for it, and its cultivation is straightforward. A farmer need do little more than clear a plot of forest from undergrowth and small trees (leaving the larger trees to provide the shade required by the cocoa tree), plant the seedlings, keep down the undergrowth with cutlasses, and wait. In five years the trees will start to bear pods and, all being well, they will continue to produce worth-while crops for another twenty years or more. The amount of capital and labour involved in the average cocoa farm is, by western standards, small. Exact figures are difficult to ascertain, but the majority of farmers would seem to be content with the income obtainable from about three to ten acres of cocoa-bearing land, producing perhaps 1,800–6,000 pounds of cocoa a year, an output which in 1954–55 gave gross incomes of between about £108 and £360 a year.[22]

In the 1880's, first missions and then the Gold Coast government began to propagate and distribute cocoa seedlings. The world demand for cocoa proved to be substantial and increasing, and its cultivation spread rapidly through the Gold Coast forest from east to west and then, from the 1920's onwards, northwards into Ashanti. Today probably about 1,200,000 acres of forest land are under cocoa. Cocoa was first exported in 1891; the value of cocoa exports first exceeded those of rubber in 1906 (£336,000, 18 per cent of all exports, compared with £334,000), and of gold in 1910 (£867,000, 33 per cent of exports, compared with £790,-000 or 30 per cent). By 1927, cocoa, at £11,728,000, accounted for nearly 83 per cent of exports, its nearest competitor being gold at £727,000 (5 per cent). The record export was in 1936, when the Gold Coast exported 311,151 tons, or 43 per cent of the world supply of cocoa. In the depression, of course, cocoa prices were low, and with the appreciation in the price of gold, Gold Coast gold production significantly increased. But even so, in 1936, cocoa exports were still worth £7,660,000 (63 per cent of exports) compared with gold exports of £3,048,000 (25 per cent).[23] In recent years, a decline in cocoa production, due principally to swollen shoot (a disease for which cutting out of infected trees is the only remedy known), has been more than offset by great increases in the world price for cocoa: in 1950 exports of cocoa totalled 267,000 tons and sold for £54,604,000, about 72 per cent of total exports.[24]

The phenomenal spread and success of cocoa as an export crop produced by small African farmers on their own farms has involved the rapid development of a money economy throughout the Gold Coast. Admittedly the new wealth and the changes brought by it are unequally spread, but they are not confined to the forest areas in the south where the cocoa is actually grown and which have gained most from the trade engendered by it. Although the staple activity of the northern savanna half of the country, which contains a quarter of the population, is still subsistence agriculture, many of its people have been attracted southwards by the wages to be gained as labourers on cocoa farms or in the many other economic activities derived to a greater or lesser extent from the success of cocoa.

The consequence has been that throughout the country, though particularly of course in its southern half, the power of money has come increasingly to erode the traditional pattern of society and the ties which held it together. In traditional society, the group, based essentially on community of kin—the family, the clan, the tribal state or nation—was always more significant than the individual. Land, property, wealth were held by the group and were used for the benefit of the group as a whole, rather than by and for the benefit of individuals, even the individuals who headed the group and determined how land and wealth should be used within it. In the last half century, more and more situations have arisen in which the individual, and *his* farm, *his* labourers, *his* land, or *his* wage-envelope and *his* savings, have begun to come first. Such individuals cannot always readily find places for themselves within the traditional groups, and so they have tended more and more to look to the examples provided by Europe and its education for new schemes of organisation, schemes as diverse as the monogamous family and political parties, football clubs and trades unions, which they could take over and shape to clothe their newly felt needs for self-expression.[25]

The extent to which the new concept of society, in which the basic unit is the individual who in different capacities may belong to any number of groups, has replaced the traditional order of groups which are inherently immutable, must not be exaggerated. It would be fallacious to suppose that the new Ghana of today is a country in which individualist concepts of society have totally eclipsed the old order of communal groups. There have been innumerable forms of compromise, even if some of them are, or will prove to be, only transitory, and the process of change has given rise to grave and fundamental problems many of which cannot be quickly or easily solved. Concepts of land tenure and testacy are in a state of flux between those sanctioned by the customary law of a communal order and those appropriate to an individualist society. An individual acquiring new wealth through his personal exertions is always in effect faced with a choice of whether he should employ some of this wealth in the traditional manner for the support of less fortunate kinsmen and for the education, and therefore the advancement, of their children, or whether he should attempt to use it for, and pass it on to, his wife and his children alone, leaving remoter relations to be supported or educated by the state with funds to which he has contributed in taxation.[26]

A similar problem was faced by the state in relation to the new wealth brought to the country by the export of cocoa. By far the greater part of government revenue comes from customs duties, which until 1916 consisted of duties on imports.[27] In that year, however, a beginning was made in levying export duties, of which that on cocoa has been by far the most significant. The rate and the yield of the export duty were both relatively low until 1950, when deliberate advantage began to be taken of the high world prices for cocoa to use the export duty as the principal means for the provision of funds for economic and social development. Three years earlier, in 1947, it had been decided that all the cocoa grown in the country should be marketed through one statutory agency, the Gold Coast Cocoa Marketing Board. The Board guarantees a price to the farmer for each season's crop, and sells in the world market for what it can get, offsetting losses if the world price is low by profits made when it is high, thus shielding the farmer from the effects of undue price fluctuations in the world market.[28] But with the high world prices for cocoa ruling since 1947, it has built up very considerable reserves over and above the income accruing to the government from export duty, and it has been able to use these not only for the benefit of the cocoa farmers, in developing grading schemes and in financing the replanting of farms devastated by swollen shoot, but also for the benefit of the community at large, in the form of grants or loans for the development of transport, education, medical, and other services.[29]

But despite expedients such as the Cocoa Marketing Board, the reconciliation of the new order and the old remains one of the major problems facing the rulers of the new Ghana, and one made none the easier by the tendency of the political opponents of the party which launched the new state to rally round traditionalist causes such as chieftaincy. Nevertheless, the tendency of the old groupings to dissolve into individuals feeling the need for new principles of coherence obviously affords a potent explanation for the rise in the Gold Coast, perhaps for the first time in Negro Africa, of a coherent, widely based nationalist political movement, and for its success in winning independence for Ghana from British colonial rule, which, until as recently as 1948, was still tending to think and act in terms more relevant to the old traditional groupings.

Constitutional Relations
Between Britain and the Gold Coast Peoples

The idea of an independent African Gold Coast, if not of a new Ghana, is one with a long pedigree which can be traced back right to the 1830's, a time when the British were very far indeed from committing themselves to any idea of a colonial or territorial government, when indeed they were thinking only in terms of negotiation with the sovereign states of the coastlands in an attempt to create a complex of local forces strong enough to ward off Ashanti. In a military sense this was achieved by the defeat of the invading Ashanti army in 1826 by a mixed force of local levies and a few Britons and Danes, but political consolidation of this victory was considered out of the question, and in 1828, indeed, the British government left the British forts to the care of the handful of British merchants, on the spot and in Britain, who were still interested in trade with the Gold Coast.

The British connection with the Gold Coast might have ended there and then, as the Danish and Dutch connections were shortly to end, had not the merchants chosen as their own particular proconsul a young Scotsman, George Maclean, who

proved to have a remarkable understanding alike of British interests on the Gold Coast and of those of the people of the native
states adjacent to the forts. In this respect Maclean stands head
and shoulders above any other chief of the British administration on the Gold Coast at any time during the nineteenth century, and their number is legion. In fact Maclean's success—and
he has a good claim to be considered the real founder of British
government on the Gold Coast—may in part be explained by
the short tenures of office and the multiplicity of policies involved in British nineteenth-century administration on the coast.
Whereas his predecessors and successors came and went with a
more than monotonous regularity at intervals at most of one or
two years (and sometimes only of a few months),[30] depending
on the exigencies of the Colonial Office and the impact of West
African diseases, and were often responsible for the affairs of
Sierra Leone and of Lagos as well as those of the Gold Coast,[31]
Maclean was able to concentrate his attention on the Gold Coast
alone for almost the whole period from 1830 to 1844; and during
this whole period of fourteen years the extent to which the Colonial Office (though not disease, for he eventually died of dysentery) could interfere with his actions and policies was filtered
by its own lack of interest in West Africa and by the fact that
Maclean was responsible, not to a succession of different Secretaries of State with varying abilities, ideas, and political interests, but to a committee of London merchants engaged in trade
with the coast.

Fundamentally, however, Maclean's success was due to his
appreciation that the interests of these merchants and of the
people of the coastal states were to a large extent identical, and
still more to the tact and patience which he brought to the implementation of policies designed to make this evident to the
African communities, communities which he set himself to understand as few other Britons of his century—whether administrators, traders, or missionaries—ever cared to do. What was
required on the Gold Coast was peace and good order, so that
British trade could prosper and increase, and so that the coastal
peoples could embark upon a course of material, political, and

moral advancement, something that was dearly needed after the ravages of slave trading and the Ashanti invasions, and which would be materially much aided by an increase of trade.

The first essential, obviously, was a firm and fair peace with Ashanti, and this Maclean, undaunted by the failure of all previous attempts, was able to negotiate shortly after his arrival on the coast. Secondly, Maclean set himself to secure orderly conditions among the coastal states for the protection of individuals and of property, so that trade and reconstruction could proceed. This he did partly by providing arbitration in disputes between states, but still more by extending into the states themselves, with the tacit consent of their rulers, some elements of British justice. In this way Maclean began to secure the eradication of local customs, such as human sacrifice, torture and barbarous punishments, panyarring (the seizure of a person or property in order to secure redress for a grievance or restitution for a debt), and other actions which he felt stood in the way of the advancement of trade and civilisation on the coast. In fact, with a revenue never exceeding about £4,000 a year and with a combined military and police force of little more than one hundred men, Maclean laid the foundations of British jurisdiction on the Gold Coast.[32]

But the extension of British jurisdiction by Maclean into territory which was not British, and over Africans who were not British subjects, had no legal foundation, and it inevitably gave rise to anomalies and irregularities which were brought to the notice of the authorities in Britain by individuals who for various reasons, usually personal spite or jealousy, were hostile to Maclean.[33] At length in 1842 Maclean's administration was enquired into by a Parliamentary Select Committee. The Committee commented very favourably on the practical advantages resulting from Maclean's activities: he had exercised "a very wholesome influence over a coast not much less than 150 miles in extent, and to a considerable distance inland, preventing within that range external slave trade, maintaining peace and security, and exercising a useful though irregular jurisdiction among the neighbouring tribes. . . ."[34] But it urged that steps should be taken to regularise this jurisdiction. Consequently in 1843 the British government decided to resume direct control of the British forts on the Gold Coast, and in 1844 a Colonial Office appointee, Captain H. W. Hill, R.N., was sent out to take over from Maclean.[35] In 1843 also, the British Parliament passed the first Foreign Jurisdiction Acts,[36] by which the British Crown received authority to exercise jurisdiction in territories beyond the formal boundaries of its sovereignty. Following these developments, Maclean was appointed the first Judicial Assessor, a kind of extra-territorial Chief Justice,[37] and a declaration was drawn up and presented by Hill to the principal coastal chiefs for their signature at a series of eleven formal meetings convened at the British forts between 6 March and 2 December 1844.

The text of this declaration was as follows:

Whereas power and jurisdiction have been exercised for and on behalf of Her Majesty the Queen of Great Britain and Ireland, within divers countries and places adjacent to Her Majesty's forts and settlements on the Gold Coast, we, Chiefs of countries and places so referred to, adjacent to the said forts and settlements, do hereby acknowledge that power and jurisdiction, and declare that the first objects of law are the protection of individuals and of property.

2. Human sacrifices, and other barbarous customs, such as pan-yarring, are abominations, and contrary to law.

3. Murders, robberies, and other crimes and offences, will be tried and inquired of before the Queen's judicial officers and the chiefs of the districts, moulding the customs of the country to the general principles of British law.[38]

This document was not a treaty, but a unilateral declaration by certain Gold Coast rulers acknowledging British jurisdiction and binding themselves to it for the future. Its historic title of "The Bond" is a correct one. The British were not contracting parties: the Bond was executed by the chiefs "*before* his Excellency the Lieutenant-Governor" and in the presence of Maclean, and the chiefs of the British military and police forces, who signed in the capacity of witnesses. In effect, the chiefs who signed the Bond were renouncing part of their sovereignty and, though this was but vaguely perceived at the time, converting their states into the semblance of a British protectorate, though one in which British authority was limited to judicial and police matters and did not legally extend into the sphere of administration. Gold Coast nationalists of the twentieth century came, with some truth, to regard the Bond as the only legal authorisation for British power on the Gold Coast.[39]

Maclean died in 1847, and thereafter, despite the Bond and its implications, the vacillations and incompetence of the Colonial Office and its local representatives rapidly destroyed the paramount position for British authority on the coast that he had created.[40] There were renewed invasions from Ashanti but no effective countermeasures from the British, the authority to whom the coastal peoples had been led to look for leadership. Trade, which under Maclean's regime had increased nearly fourfold (1831: exports £70,000, imports £131,000; 1840: exports £325,000, imports £423,000), fell off sharply (1864: exports £171,000, imports £166,000). In 1865, the British interest in West Africa was the subject of another Parliamentary enquiry, and the British government decided to withdraw altogether from the Gold Coast as soon as it could reasonably get out of its existing commitments: the object of British policy was to be "to encourage in the natives the exercise of those qualities which may render it possible for us more and more to transfer to them the administration [of government] with a view to our ultimate withdrawal. . . ."[41]

In this connection, despite the abandonment of the political paramountcy for Britain that had been fostered by Maclean's work, the influence of the latter was still to be felt. It combined with that of the new social forces engendered by European trade and education to bring together educated men from the Fante states to organise a national system of government in which they and the traditional chiefs could join together to take over as the British withdrew. In 1871, the Fante Confederation met at Mankesim and produced a constitution.[42]

But almost simultaneously, as we have seen,[43] the final departure of the Dutch occasioned an abrupt reversal of British policy, so abrupt in fact that the authors of the Mankesim Constitution were for a space treated by the British officials on the coast as traitors to the Queen, the British queen, to whom in fact the chiefs and people of the Gold Coast states had never owed allegiance! [44]

This tragicomical situation was, however, cut short when, on 24 July 1874, shortly after the British expedition against Ashanti, the Gold Coast was proclaimed a British colony. This step was an abrupt check to the aspirations of the intellectual elite on the coast, who, from the Bond onwards and especially after 1865, had been led to think of Britain in the light of a guardian who would relinquish her trusteeship as soon as her ward was educated and prosperous enough to stand in the world on her own feet. But the disillusionment of the elite was only temporary. Its members soon realised that the emergent British administration needed for the new colony after 1874 offered many opportunities for their employment as administrative, medical, technical officers and the like, and some of them began to rise in it to senior posts. They began to conceive that self-government for the Gold Coast would come about inevitably in course of time through the Africanisation of the personnel of the British colonial government.

Yet once again the course of events combined to frustrate the expectations of the elite. As has already been mentioned, in the 1890's, Britain began to take her colonial responsibilities seriously. Colonial government began to be extended to Ashanti and to the Northern Territories, regions to which little or no European influence had hitherto reached, and whose assimilation to the level of development of the coastal colony would necessarily delay the advance of the latter towards the self-government which was the goal of its elite. Furthermore, these extensive new territories necessitated a considerable enlargement of the colonial administration at the same time as its extension into technical spheres of economic and social development and control involved new standards of recruitment. Thus, while the numbers of officers in the senior grades of government service began to increase considerably, both the number and the proportion of locally recruited senior staff began to decline. The personnel of the administration became overwhelmingly European, a process that was accelerated by the contemporary development of the Colonial Service into a body of men available for service anywhere within the greatly enlarged British empire.[45]

The coastal elite had consequently to seek a new ground on which to fight for self-government. It was aided in its choice by the need to protect African interests from invasion by Europeans seeking forest land for mining and for timber concessions. There were individuals only too ready to grant such concessions for immediate cash even if their own right to dispose of the land in question was none too sure, which might well be the case if, as often happened, the land was the property of a group rather than of individuals. Desiring to provide some security for the investment of European capital in Gold Coast lands, and in some degree to avoid the underlying conflict between individual and communal notions of land ownership, the Gold Coast government proposed in the 1890's to apply the conceptions of Crown or public land to all unoccupied land in the colony. This led to a storm of protest in which the coastal lawyers, who stood to lose much of their business in the negotiation of concessions and in law suits over land the title to which was not well defined, joined with the traditional rulers in asserting that all land in the colony, whether occupied or not, was the land of some group or individual. The Lands Bill was eventually dropped,[46] but out of the agitation against it had developed a permanent political association, the Aborigines' Rights Protection Society, dominated by the African lawyers and businessmen of Cape Coast and Sekondi, but standing for the assertion and maintenance of the rights of the coastal chiefs, their states and people.[47]

The political aim of this association became the democratisation of the local colonial legislature, the Legislative Council.[48] A Legislative Council had been instituted in the Gold Coast in 1850 to provide the governor with a formal means of taking account of local opinion when enacting legislation for the colony and drawing up its budget. With the governor as president, it consisted initially of two of his senior officials and two nominated "gentlemen," that is to say persons not connected with the administration. One of the founder members of the Council was the notable mulatto merchant, James Bannerman, who in 1850–51 indeed, when acting as governor, was the first president of the Council. The first full-blooded African member, G. K. Blankson, another merchant, was appointed in 1861. By 1901, the Council consisted of the governor, four officials, the chief justice, and four nominated unofficials, two of them Africans, one of whom, J. M. Sarbah, a barrister, had been one of the most skilful protagonists against the projected lands legislation of the 1890's.[49]

The ambition of the elite was to secure the conversion of the Legislative Council into a body in which African unofficial members would be in the majority, and would be chosen by an African electorate instead of being nominated by the governor. In this way the activities of the colonial administration would be subject to the control of African representatives, and from representative government it was hoped that it would be a short step to responsible government, in which the executive would not be responsible to the governor, and through him to the Secretary of State for the Colonies answerable only to the British Parliament, but to the elected representatives of a Gold Coast electorate.[50]

In 1916 the Legislative Council was reconstituted to include nine nominated unofficials, six of them Africans, as opposed to eleven officials and the governor, and then, between 1919 and 1927, a new governor, Sir Gordon Guggisberg, went far towards creating a new political climate in which it began to seem possible that the ambitions of the elite might shortly be achieved. Guggisberg was a remarkable man with a flair for inspiring the trust and respect of the Gold Coast African unequalled by any governor since Maclean. By profession he was an army engineer, and in the early years of the twentieth century, he had served as an officer in the Gold Coast survey and had thus come into closer contact with the people of the country than many officials and had got to know them well.[51] When he ended the war of 1914–18 as an unemployed brigadier-general, his conviction that the Gold Coast people were not getting a square deal from the colonial officials of the time, whom he regarded as hopelessly limited in outlook and purpose, was strong enough to enable him to secure his appointment to the governorship of the colony. Guggisberg's programme for the Gold Coast was farseeing and comprehensive: the active development of the economy through the improvement and expansion of its transport system; the improvement of the health of its people by the provision of better medical services; the development of its education system so that it would produce academically and technically trained men and women of high standard to Africanise all branches of government services and to provide leaders in all walks of life; and the democratisation of municipal government and of the Legislative Council.

Guggisberg's plans were aided by the buoyant condition of the country's economy during his period of office. The boom years of 1919–20 and steady prosperity after 1923 provided the financial resources needed to convert his drive and purpose into concrete reality. In this respect, indeed, he was lucky; some of his predecessors in office had been handicapped primarily by shortage of funds, and not, as Guggisberg supposed, by lack of purpose and imagination. This was particularly the case, perhaps, with his immediate predecessor, Sir Hugh Clifford (1912–19),[52] whose activities were necessarily restricted by wartime stringencies. Many of Guggisberg's most tangible achievements —Takoradi harbour, the Gold Coast's first deepwater port, Achimota College, which Guggisberg and its first principal and vice-principal, Rev. A. G. Fraser and Dr. J. E. K. Aggrey, planned with remarkable success as a coeducational institution which would provide an education to the degree level second to none in quality and character,[53] and the Gold Coast hospital at Korlebu, at the time of its completion the finest hospital in Negro Africa—would hardly have been possible financially before the 1920's. However, Guggisberg did have a remarkable flair for doing what articulate African opinion considered necessary. Although in the political sphere his autocratic conviction that he knew best what was best for the country was apt to lead

to difficulties—his municipal reforms were stillborn and his reform of the Legislative Council did not have the results he expected from it—his governorship is still remembered with respect and affection.[54]

Guggisberg—and here again the parallel with Maclean is evident—wanted to work through and with the traditional institutions of the country. Accordingly he created provincial councils
of chiefs which were to be forums for the expression of African
opinion and which were also to serve as electoral colleges choos-
ing six of the unofficial members of the Legislative Council.
There were also to be three African unofficial members elected
by the ratepayers of the three principal towns of the Gold Coast
colony,[55] and five nominated European unofficials. As against
these fourteen unofficial members, nine of whom were Africans,
the government side of the Legislative Council was enlarged to
include fifteen officials besides the governor. But this reform did
not meet with the approval of the educated elite. This was in
part due to the fact that under the leadership of J. E. Casely
Hayford, a barrister, who, after the death of Sarbah in 1910, had
been the leading personality in the movement centred round the
Aborigines' Rights Protection Society,[56] some of them had moved
on to contemplate much wider ambitions. In 1918, Casely Hayford left the Aborigines' Rights Protection Society and founded
the National Congress of (British) West Africa, which for some
years sought, without success, to influence the British government at home to grant to all the West African colonies complete
representative government.[57] But this did not meet with the approval of the chiefly classes of the Gold Coast, and Guggisberg's
system of provincial councils of chiefs, electing the bulk of the
elected members of the Legislative Council, together with the
failure of his scheme for a measure of municipal self-government,
served still further to widen the breach between the chiefs and
the urban intelligentsia. Guggisberg thus seemed to take the
traditional authorities into partnership with the colonial government at the expense of the European-educated classes. The alliance of the 1890's was thus disrupted, and the educated elite

began to regard the chiefs increasingly as agents of the colonial administration which they aimed to destroy.

Less inspiring successors at Government House, the economic depression of the 1930's, and the restrictions of the war years 1939–45 combined to dim the new light which Guggisberg had brought to Gold Coast affairs. When the war years began to recede, and left in their wake a new and active British approach towards problems of colonial advancement and economic development,[58] it rapidly transpired that in the Gold Coast this new approach was hopelessly outdated.

In 1946, at the instigation of Sir Alan Burns, governor from 1941 to 1947, who in 1942 had appointed two Africans to his executive council and who had since 1943 engaged in numerous consultations with local political leaders, the Gold Coast received a new constitution. In the Legislative Council for the first time British officials were outnumbered, not only by unofficial members, but by African representatives. Admittedly not all of the African majority was elected, and of those that were, thirteen were elected by the Councils of Chiefs compared with five elected directly by urban electorates.[59] But the 1946 constitution embodied much of the programme of the nationalists of the 1920's, and it was everywhere hailed by informed British opinion as a bold leap forward. Yet two years later there were serious political disturbances in the larger towns of the colony, and the subsequent commission of enquiry (chairman: Mr. Aiken Watson, K.C.) reported unequivocally, and with exemplary speed, that the 1946 constitution "was outmoded at birth" and recommended the establishment of a constitution in which much of the business of government should be the responsibility of African ministers responsible to a predominantly elective assembly.[60] In 1949, the details of such a constitution were worked out by a committee appointed by the governor from among the leading members of the African community, and presided over by an African judge, Mr. J. Henley Coussey.[61] In 1951, a constitution based on the Coussey Committee's recommendations came into force,[62] and the Gold Coast was launched on a transitory period of limited responsible government which led rapidly and remarkably smoothly to the complete independence of British control achieved by the new Ghana in 1957.

In essentials, what had happened so radically to change the political situation was that the frustration of the Gold Coast elite had been reinforced by a new and much more explosive frustration, the frustration, if not quite of the masses, of a vast new class of individuals emancipated, or seeking emancipation, from the leading strings of the traditional communal order of society—clerks, storekeepers, mechanics, cocoa farmers, schoolteachers, and young men straight from school who were still adrift between two worlds. The numbers and the horizons of this class had been greatly extended by the effects of World War II. Many of them saw armed service abroad, particularly in southeast Asia; still more had acquired new skills, new knowledge, and a new outlook in military service nearer home. In all, over 65,000 Gold Coast Africans experienced military service of some kind, an appreciable proportion of a population which at the outbreak of war was less than four million. It is significant that the disturbances of 1948 were set off by incidents arising out of a veterans' demonstration.[63] Even if perhaps the majority of this new class had not seen military service, the war had brought them new employments and wages, had shown them white men of the Royal Air Force and the U.S. Services engaged in working with their hands and acting in countless other ways disruptive of the old myth of the Europeans as a superior class ordained only to direct and rule,[64] and had brought talk of the Atlantic Charter [65] and of a new British approach to colonial problems, including the Colonial Development and Welfare Act of 1945 which made £120,000,000 available for economic and social development in the colonies over the next ten years.

But in the first years of peace, the expectations of this new semi-elite were dashed to the ground. There was a continued shortage of the consumer goods to which they felt entitled, and prices soared. A shortage of capital goods helped to delay the implementation of schemes of economic development and social improvement. The gulf which had developed since c. 1900 between the European administration and the bulk of the African people, a gulf all too obvious to Clifford and Guggisberg, but which neither of them had permanently managed to bridge, seemed to be widening rather than closing.[66] The Gold Coast did not become the new heaven that was expected; it became a new purgatory in which the sought-after new opportunities, wages, standards, rights, seemed to diminish rather than to increase.

Here at last was the opportunity for the old elite. In 1947, the United Gold Coast Convention had been founded. Its leading spirit was Dr. J. B. Danquah, another lawyer in the tradition of J. M. Sarbah and Casely Hayford, who in the constitutional discussions of the later war years had come to the fore as an advocate of a popular assembly and ministerial government. Disappointed with the Burns constitution, Danquah began to appeal beyond the narrow circle of the old elite. The old polite contest with government fought according to gentlemanly conventions derived from British politics of the nineteenth century went overboard; the citadels were now to be forced with the new twentieth-century weapon of mass discontent. The United Gold Coast Convention became the first real political *party* (as opposed to political *associations*) in Gold Coast history, appealing directly to the people with a programme of self-government at the earliest possible opportunity. It was Danquah who, looking for a banner under which to organise mass support, hit on the idea of reviving the traditions of a connection between the Gold Coast and the earliest known West African Negro empire so as to break with the colonial past: the new state was to be Ghana.[67] It was also Danquah, who, needing new blood to organise the new movement, invited Dr. Kwame Nkrumah, a young man who in 1935 had gone abroad to study at Lincoln University, the University of Pennsylvania, and in London, to return to the Gold Coast as organising secretary of the U.G.C.C.

The U.G.C.C. made such effective capital of the 1948 disturbances that Danquah, Nkrumah, and four of their colleagues were for a time deported and placed under detention in the Northern Territories. When, after their release, the Coussey

Committee was announced, Nkrumah objected to the manner in which its members had been selected by government nomination.[68] Danquah, on the other hand, together with some other leading members of the U.G.C.C., took part in the Committee's deliberations. Here was a parting of the ways. While Danquah was occupied, from January to August, 1949, in the Coussey Committee, collaborating in the working out of a constitution which, however far it went in the right direction, still fell appreciably short of his party's goal of full self-government, Nkrumah was free to pursue his political activities.[69] An extremely able orator and a first-class politician, who proved closer than Danquah to the public pulse, he sensed that the masses he had organised would follow a leader who declared himself against any compromise. In June, 1949, he finally broke with the U.G.C.C. and founded his own party, the Convention People's Party, whose slogan was "Self Government Now," and which was soon able to brand the Coussey Commission as "bogus." Nkrumah's political judgment was wholly apt: the U.G.C.C. soon became a middle-class liberal rump whose thunder had been stolen by Nkrumah's clear-cut radical aggression and persuasive oratory. The masses went with the C.P.P. Their support became even more wholehearted in 1950 when, as the result of a campaign of "Positive Action"—strikes and semiviolent actions designed to force the government into an immediate grant of self-government—their leader and his principal lieutenants received prison sentences for sedition. The hero had become a martyr for the cause.

In February, 1951, the first general election was held for the Legislative Assembly under the Coussey constitution. Of the thirty-eight seats in the Assembly which were open to popular election, the C.P.P. won thirty-four, the U.G.C.C. only three. In the urban constituencies, the C.P.P. majority was overwhelming. In Accra, Nkrumah, still in jail, received 22,780 votes out of 23,122 cast.[70] The governor, Sir Charles Arden-Clarke, who had arrived in the country in August, 1949, was equal to the situation. Nkrumah was released from jail, together with other principal members of the C.P.P., and at a momentous interview was invited to become Leader of Government Business, a post equivalent to Prime Minister, a title which was accorded him in 1952. Nkrumah accepted and took office at the head of a ministry dominated by C.P.P. members. Thus began a remarkable working partnership between Nkrumah and his C.P.P. colleagues and Arden-Clarke and the senior British officials, which, through the exercise of tact and political acumen on both sides, secured the gradual transformation of the Coussey constitution into a system of full parliamentary government completely independent of Westminster.

This change was not achieved without opposition, but this came not from the British authorities,[71] but principally from the more conservative and traditionalist elements in indigenous society, in Ashanti especially, and to some extent also in the Northern Territories and in Togoland. But this opposition was of necessity particularist, and it proved unable to organise on a nation-wide basis effectively enough to resist a centralised, popular party which was so evidently succeeding with its programme of independence for the people as a whole. This C.P.P. policy and Nkrumah's leadership were confirmed by general elections in 1954 and 1956, both of which gave the C.P.P. some seventy per cent of the seats in the Legislative Assembly. The process of transition from colonial status to full independence was completed on 6 March 1957,[72] the hundred and third anniversary of the Bond, when the Gold Coast became Ghana, a new state which was at once accepted as a free and independent member of the United Nations as well as of the British Commonwealth.

Notes | *Index*

Notes

Abbreviations Used in the Notes

TGCTHS: Transactions of the Gold Coast and Togoland Historical Society
THSG: Transactions of the Historical Society of Ghana

Chapter I

1   On the geography of West Africa generally, see R. J. Harrison Church, *West Africa: A Study of the Environment and of Man's Use of It* (London: Longmans, 1957). On Ghana in particular, see E. A. Boateng, *A Geography of Ghana* (Cambridge University Press, 1958), or W. J. Varley and H. P. White, *The Geography of Ghana* (London: Longmans, 1958).
2   A handy reference book on the languages of West Africa is Diedrich Westermann and M. A. Bryan, *Languages of West*

Africa ("Handbook of African Languages," Part II [London: Oxford University Press for International African Institute, 1952]). The classification of Westermann and Bryan now needs to be reviewed in the light of J. H. Greenberg, *Studies in African Linguistic Classification* (New Haven: Compass Publishing Co., 1955). The terminology used here is that of Westermann and Bryan.

3 For the views of a leading social anthropologist on this theme, see Daryll Forde, "The Cultural Map of West Africa: Successive Adaptations to Tropical Forests and Grasslands," *Transactions of the New York Academy of Science*, Ser. 2, XV (1953), 206–19.

4 See, for example, Raymond Mauny, "Autour de la répartition des chars rupestres du Nord-Ouest Africain," *Actes du Congrès Panafricain de Préhistorie*, IIe Session, Alger, 1952 (Paris: Arts et Métiers Graphiques, 1955), pp. 741–46. It is noteworthy that the lines along which the main concentrations of engravings of carts occur correspond in general terms with the areas of the Sahara which afford solid going, and so also with those in which the main camel caravan routes later developed (and the present-day motor *pistes*). Mauny seems in no doubt that the purpose of the carts was commerce. On the other hand H. Lhote, e.g., his *Les Touaregs du Hoggar* (2nd ed.; Paris: Payot, 1955), pp. 68–72, would seem to view them primarily as evidence of the military expansion towards the Niger of Libyan peoples to be associated with the Garamantes recorded by Herodotus. Unfortunately the French word *char* covers both "cart" and "chariot."

5 See, for example, E. F. Gautier, *The Sahara*, trans. D. F. Mayhew (New York: Columbia University Press, 1935). Gautier's works have become classics in many fields, but for those who prefer more modern authorities, see Robert Capot-Rey, *Le Sahara Français* (Paris: Presses Universitaires de France, 1953), Chap. 3, and H. Alimen, *The Prehistory of Africa*, trans. A. H. Brodrick (London: Hutchinson, 1957), pp. 138–39.

6 As late as the tenth and eleventh centuries, the Berber Sanhaja tribes of southern Mauretania were disputing the mastery of the region with the essentially Negro state of Ghana. On the vexed question of the antiquity of the Negro in the Sahara, see a useful short discussion of the evidence in Lhote, *Touaregs*, pp. 76–78. In the east, a Negro people seems to have been definitely living as far north as Khartoum before 2300 B.C.—A. J. Arkell, *A History of the Sudan to 1821* (London: Athlone Press, 1955), pp. 24–28.

7   It must not be supposed that the Sahara was not traversable by
    man before the camel became available; the evidence of the
    rock engravings is clear that horses were used in the desert, if
    not for trade, certainly for military purposes, long before the
    camel was introduced.—Lhote, *Touaregs*, pp. 76–78. Some
    genera of horse seem to be at least as old in northwestern Africa
    as man. See Alimen, *Prehistory*, pp. 23, 29. It is probable that
    the bullock was also in use for Saharan transport in the pre-
    camel era.—E. W. Bovill, *The Golden Trade of the Moors*
    (London: Oxford University Press, 1958), pp. 16–18. But it was
    the coming of the camel which made possible a vast increase
    in the scale and permanence of human movements across the
    desert, whether movements of trade or of migration. The literature
    on the introduction of the camel into northwest Africa is con-
    siderable, but see O. Brogan, "The Camel in Roman Tripolitania,"
    Papers of the British School at Rome, XXII (1954); E. F.
    Gautier, *The Sahara*, Chap. 10, and his *Le passé de l'Afrique
    du Nord; les siècles obscurs* (Paris: Payot, 1952 ed.), pp. 188–
    244; Bovill, *Golden Trade*, pp. 41–43, 48–49. On the camel
    in Saharan rock engravings, see Lhote, *Touaregs*, pp. 74–75.

8   See pp. 39–40 below.

9   See Bovill, *Golden Trade*, Chaps. 15, 16, 17; also his articles
    "The Moorish Invasion of the Sudan," *Journal of the African
    Society*, XXVI (1926), 245–62 and 380–87, and XXVII (1927),
    47–56.

10 On the Egyptians in the Sudan, see Richard Hill, *Egypt in the
    Sudan, 1820–81* (Oxford: Clarendon Press, 1959); also Mekki
    Shibeika, *British Policy in the Sudan 1882–1902* (London: Ox-
    ford University Press, 1952), Introductory Chapter, which is
    based on a longer work of the author's in Arabic.

11 See J. Spencer Trimingham, *Islam in the Sudan* (London: Oxford
    University Press, 1949), especially Chap. 2, and Arkell, *History
    of the Sudan*, Chaps. 8 and 9.

12 There is a useful monograph on the people of Tibesti by Walter
    Cline, *The Teda of Tibesti* ("General Series in Anthropology,"
    No. 12 [Menasha, Wisconsin: 1950]). For a short general dis-
    cussion on the early populations of the Sahara, see L. Cabot
    Briggs, "Living Tribes of the Sahara and the Problem of Their
    Prehistoric Origins," *Proceedings of the Third Pan-African Con-
    gress on Prehistory*, Livingstone, 1955 (London: Chatto and
    Windus, 1957), pp. 195–99.

13 On the Arab conquest of North Africa in general, C. H. Becker's
    chapter in *Cambridge Medieval History*, II (1913), 366–90,

is probably still the best general survey in English. On the conquest of Egypt and its effect on its inhabitants, see S. Lane-Poole, *A History of Egypt in the Middle Ages* (2nd ed.; London: Methuen, 1914), Chaps. 1–3. A stimulating discussion of the Arab conquest of the Maghrib and its consequences is that to be found in Gautier, *Le passé de l'Afrique du Nord,* Book IV, while a good outline, involving a critical approach to Gautier's ideas, is to be found in C. A. Julien, *Histoire de l'Afrique du Nord,* ed. R. Le Tourneau (2nd ed. rev.; Paris: Payot, 1952), II, Chaps. 1–3.

14   For one description of the mechanism of infiltration into the Sudan by transhumants from the north, see Y. Urvoy, *Histoire des populations du Soudan central* (Paris: Larose, 1936), pp. 144–45, 151–52.

15   Jean Rouch, *Contribution à l'histoire du Songhay* ("Mémoires de l'Institut Français d'Afrique Noire," No. 29 [Dakar: 1953]), pp. 169–70.

16   For the Abuyazidu legends, see H. R. Palmer, *Sudanese Memoirs* (Lagos: Govt. Printer, 1928), III, 132–63, and Urvoy, *Histoire des populations,* pp. 225–30. On Abu Yazid's revolt in the eastern Maghrib, see, for example, Julien, *Histoire de l'Afrique du Nord,* II, 62–64.

17   See J. P. Lebeuf and A. Masson Detourbet, *La civilisation du Tchad* (Paris: Payot, 1950).

18   The best general guide to the history of the western Sudan is E. W. Bovill, *Caravans of the Old Sahara* (London: Oxford University Press, 1933). This is scarce, but it is not wholly superseded by his rewritten version, *The Golden Trade of the Moors,* published by the same press in 1958. For the central Sudan, the best guide is probably still Urvoy's *Histoire des populations,* now to be supplemented by the same author's *Histoire de l'empire du Bornou* ("Mémoires de l'Institut Français d'Afrique Noire," No. 7 [Paris: Larose, 1949]).

19   J. Richard-Molard, *Afrique Occidentale Française* (2nd ed.; Paris: Berger-Levrault, 1952), pp. 195–96.

20   See, for example, Arkell, *History of the Sudan,* pp. 106–7.

21   See, for example, Raymond Mauny, "Notes on the Protohistoric Period in West Africa," *Journal of the West African Science Association,* II, Part 2 (August, 1956), 207–8, and the list of authorities quoted in n. 11; also A. A. Kwapong, "Africa Antiqua," *TGCTHS,* II, Part 2 (1956), 3–5.

22   Bovill, *Caravans,* p. 61.

23   Maçoudi (Ali ibn Husain, al-Mas'ūdī), *Les prairies d'or,* trans. and ed. by B. de Meynard and P. de Courteilles (Paris: Im-

primerie impériale, 1861–77), IV, 92–93; Yāqūt ibn 'Abd Allāh al-Ḥamawī, *Jacut's geographische Wörterbuch*, trans. and ed. by F. Wüstenfeld (Leipzig: Brockhaus, 1866–69); and Herodotus, Book IV, 196.

24 The relevant sections of these and other Arabic authorities, such as Yaqut, to which reference is made in these pages may be found conveniently grouped together, with a parallel translation into French, in Yusuf Kamal, *Monumenta Cartographica Africae et Aegypti* (Cairo: 1926–38). Thus Al Fazari is in Vol. III, fasc. 1, p. 510; Al Yaqubi, *ibid.*, pp. 519–25; Al Mas'udi, Vol. III, fasc. 2, pp. 625–29; Idrisi, Vol. III, fasc. 4, pp. 827–45; Yaqut, Vol. III, fasc. 5, pp. 948–64.

25 Maurice Delafosse, *Haut-Sénégal-Niger* (3 vols.; Paris: Larose, 1912), I, 55; Bovill, *Golden Trade*, pp. 192–201.

26 Two chronicles written at Timbuctu in the sixteenth and seventeenth centuries, the *Tarikh el-Fettach* by Mahmoud Kati, trans. and ed. O. Houdas and M. Delafosse (Paris: Leroux, 1913), and the *Tarikh es-Soudan* by Es-Sa'di, trans. and ed. O. Houdas (Paris: Leroux, 1900), report these traditions for Gao and also say something of them for Ghana. The latter have been discussed by Raymond Mauny, "The Question of Ghana," *Africa*, XXIV, No. 3 (July, 1954), 200–212, and the former by Rouch, *Contribution à l'histoire du Songhay*, pp. 169–73. For Hausa and Bornu traditions, see Palmer, *Sudanese Memoirs*, *passim*, and for discussions of them see Urvoy, *Histoire des populations*, pp. 222–29 and *Histoire de l'empire*, pp. 21–30.

27 The relatively scanty information available for Ghana is summarised in J. D. Fage, "Ghana: A Review of the Evidence," *THSG*, III, Part 2 (1957), 77–98, as well as in Mauny's article in *Africa* (July, 1954), pp. 200–212. The best source for Mali is Charles Monteil, "Les empires de Mali," *Bulletin du Comité d'Etudes Historiques et Scientifiques de l'Afrique Occidentale Française*, XII (1929), 291–447; and for the Songhai empire of Gao, Rouch, *Contribution à l'histoire du Songhay*.

28 See, *inter alia*, Bovill, *Golden Trade*, pp. 67–68, 140–41, 236–37.

29 Rouch, *Contribution à l'histoire du Songhay*, pp. 192–204.

30 Joseph Dupuis, *Journal of a Residence in Ashantee* (London: H. Colburn, 1824), especially pp. 94–97, vi–xv, and Appendices 4–11.

31 Eva L. R. Meyerowitz, *Akan Traditions of Origin* (London: Faber, 1952), pp. 34–35, and *The Akan of Ghana* (London: Faber, 1958), p. 107.

32 Meyerowitz, *Akan Traditions*, pp. 45–48, and *The Akan of*

Ghana, p. 115; also Jack Goody, "A Note on the Penetration of Islam into the West of the Northern Territories of the Gold Coast," *TGCTHS,* I, Part 2 (1953), 45–46.

33   "The Kano Chronicle," reign of Yakubu, in Palmer, *Sudanese Memoirs,* III, 92–132.

34   [H. A. Blair and A. Duncan-Johnstone], *Enquiry into the Constitution and Organisation of the Dagbon Kingdom* (Accra: Govt. Printer, 1932), p. 49, and E. Forster Tamakloe, *Brief History of the Dagbamba People* (Accra: Govt. Printer, 1931). Tamakloe dates Zangina 1643–77, but there is evidence to show that this is at least fifty years too early; see, e.g., comment in W. E. F. Ward, *A History of the Gold Coast* (London: Allen & Unwin, 1948), p. 121, n. 73 (new edition, 1958, entitled *A History of Ghana*).

35   In Kano, for example, in the reign of Yaji, 1349–85. For a general statement of Wangara, i.e., Mande, influence in Hausaland, see Urvoy, *Histoire des populations,* pp. 230–31.

36   For the traditions of origin of the Gold Coast peoples generally, see Meyerowitz, *Akan Traditions,* and Ward, *Gold Coast,* especially Chaps. 2, 3, and 6. For Dagomba, see Blair and Duncan-Johnstone, *Constitution and Organisation,* and Tamakloe, *Brief History.* The latter is also printed as Chap. 11 of A. W. Cardinall, *Tales Told in Togoland* (London: Oxford University Press, 1931). There are a number of available versions of Mossi tradition. That given in Leo Frobenius, *The Voice of Africa,* trans. Rudolf Blind (London: Hutchinson, 1913), Chap. 23, is perhaps the most useful, though reference should also be made to Delafosse, *Haut-Sénégal-Niger,* II, Chap. 4, and Louis Tauxier, *Le noir de Yatenga* (Paris: Larose, 1917), and *Nouvelles notes sur le Mossi et le Gourounsi* (Paris: Larose, 1924). Delafosse's dating should be disregarded. Mamprussi tradition is but imperfectly known; there is little in print other than the version in R. S. Rattray, *Tribes of the Ashanti Hinterland* (London: Oxford University Press, 1932), II, Chap. 59.

37   On Gonja tradition, see the material in Jack Goody, *The Ethnography of the Northern Territories of the Gold Coast West of the White Volta* (London: Colonial Office, 1954), and Meyerowitz, *Akan Traditions,* Chap. 3.

38   This subject is currently being investigated at length by Mr. Ivor Wilks of the University College of Ghana.

39   On Gã and Ewe traditions generally, see Ward, *Gold Coast,* especially pp. 51–52, 97–100, and 126–29. For Gã tradition, see M. J. Field, *Social Organisation of the Gã People* (London:

Crown Agents, 1940), and C. C. Reindorf, *The History of the Gold Coast and Asante* (Basel: originally published 1895, later reprint n.d.); for Adangme, see *Nene* Azu Mate Kole, "The Historical Background of Krobo Customs," *TGCTHS*, I, Part 4 (1955), 133–40; for Ewe, see résumé by D. H. Jones, in *History and Archaeology in Africa* (London: School of Oriental and African Studies, 1955), pp. 59–62, and works there listed in bibliography on p. 87.

40 See, for example, Jacob U. Egharevba, *A Short History of Benin* (2nd ed.; Benin: 1953), p. 13.

41 See E. G. Parrinder, *The Story of Ketu* (Ibadan: University Press, 1956).

42 The modern authority is M. J. Herskovits, *Dahomey* (2 vols.; New York: Augustin, 1938). See also the short historical résumé by D. H. Jones, in *History and Archaeology in Africa,* pp. 62–64.

43 S. O. Biobaku, *The Lugard Lectures, 1955* (Lagos: Federal Information Services, 1955), p. 21.

44 See the article by Fage, "Ghana: A Review," *THSG*, III, Part 2, 77–98; also Meyerowitz, *Akan Traditions,* especially pp. 124–29, and her article, "The Akan and Ghana," *Man* (June, 1957), 99, and the article by Mauny in *Africa* (July, 1954), pp. 200–212.

45 Westermann and Bryan, *Languages of West Africa,* p. 31.

46 These conclusions *re* Dagomba are based on work by the late Dr. David Tait and the author, some of it as yet unpublished. However, see David Tait, "History and Social Observation," *TGCTHS,* I, Part 5 (1955), 193–210. The most relevant of the many articles by Dr. Tait on the Konkomba is "The Political System of Konkomba," *Africa,* XXIII, No. 3 (July, 1953), 213–23.

47 L. G. Binger, *Du Niger au Golfe de Guinée* (Paris: Hachette, 1893), I, 370, 482, 491–92; II, 38–39.

48 Mossi tradition refers to their ancestor Yennenga (female) marrying Riale, a Mande hunter; Dagomba tradition has their first ancestors rendering aid to the "King of Melle."

49 Compare, for example, the Lwoo invasions of what is now Uganda, as discussed recently by Roland Oliver, "The Traditional Histories of Buganda, Bunyoro, and Nkole," *Journal of the Royal Anthropological Institute,* LXXXV (1955), 111–17, or the "conquering hordes sweeping across the land to establish an ephemeral empire over other small states or over tribes without state-like organisations," postulated by Professor Max Gluckman for a central African environment less conducive to political stability in his "Anthropology in Central Africa," *Journal of the Royal Society of Arts,* CIII (1955), 645–65, at p. 649.

50   This conclusion was I think first stated by Mr. Ward, *Gold Coast,*
pp. 34–36, and has since been substantiated by Mrs. Meyerowitz's
Akan Traditions.

51   Any new state composed of distinct kinship groups, each with a
ritual lien on the land it occupies, must seek to replace their
disparate traditions by one of its own which asserts its own right-
ful ownership to the land. Hence, for example, the Ashanti statement that their people came out of the ground at Asantemanso.
See Ward, *Gold Coast,* pp. 54–56.

52   See Biobaku, *Lugard Lectures,* p. 21. Reference has already been
made to the Bayajidda or Abuyazidu legends. See above, p. 12
and n. 16. For the Kisra legends, see A. B. Mathews, "The Kisra
Legend," *African Studies,* IX (1950), 144–47, as well as Palmer,
Sudanese Memoirs, II, 61–63. The Yoruba version of the Oduduwa legend is given by Biobaku; the Benin version by Egha-
verba, *Short History of Benin.*

Chapter II

1   M. G. De Slane, *Description de l'Afrique septentrionale par
Abou-Obeid-el-Bekri* (2nd ed., 2 vols.; Algiers: Jourdan, 1911–
13), I, 328–31.

2   R. Dozy and M. J. De Goeje, *Idrisi, description de l'Afrique* (2
vols.; Leyden: 1866).

3   Ibn Khaldoun, *Histoire des Berbères et des dynasties musulmanes
de l'Afrique septentrionale,* trans. M. G. De Slane, new ed. by
P. Casanova (4 vols.; Paris: Geuthner, 1925–56); Ibn Khaldun,
The Muqaddimah: An Introduction to History, trans. and ed.
F. Rosenthal (3 vols.; London: Routledge, 1958); Charles Issawi,
An Arab Philosophy of History (London: Murray, 1950). The
full significance of Ibn Khaldun's work has tended to be obscured
from western eyes by the piecemeal manner in which it has been
translated from the Arabic. What we generally know as the
Prolegomena (*Muqaddimah*) and the *History of the Berbers*
are in fact sections of one great work, the full title of which may
be translated as *Instructive Examples from, and Collected Origins
and Accounts of, the History of the Arabs, Foreign Peoples, and
the Berbers.*

4   Jean-Léon l'Africain, *Description de l'Afrique,* trans. A. Epaulard
and annotated by A. Epaulard, Th. Monod, H. Lhote, and
R. Mauny (2 vols.; Paris: Adrien-Maisonneuve, 1956).

5   See G. H. T. Kimble, *Geography in the Middle Ages* (London:
Methuen, 1938), Chap. 5.

6 Louis de Mas Latrie, *Relations et commerce de l'Afrique sep-tentrionale ou Maghreb avec les nations chrétiennes* (Paris: 1886); A. E. Sayous, *Le commerce des Européens à Tunis depuis le XIIe siècle jusqu'à la fin du XVIe siècle* (Paris: Société d'Editions Geographiques, Maritimes et Coloniales, 1929).

7 The best source for these journeys, and for early European knowledge of and relations with the western Sudan generally, is Charles De la Roncière, *La découverte de l'Afrique au moyen âge* ("Mémoires de la Société Royale de Géographie d'Egypte," V, VI, and XIII [Cairo: 1924–27]).

8 Herodotus, Book IV, 42. See comment on the feasibility of this and other reported ancient African voyages in J. Holland Rose, *Man and the Sea* (Cambridge: Heffer, 1935).

9 On the Vivaldi expedition, see De la Roncière, *La découverte de l'Afrique*, I, Chap. 2, and Alberto Magnaghi, *Precursori di Colombo? Il tentativo di viaggio transoceanico dei Genovesi fratelli Vivaldi nel 1291* ("Memorie della Reale società geografica italiana," XVIII [Rome: 1935]).

10 De la Roncière, *La découverte de l'Afrique*, especially I, Chaps. 1, 5, and 7, and II, Chap. 3; C. R. Beazley, *The Dawn of Modern Geography* (London: H. Frowde, 1906), III, especially p. 376 to end; Kimble, *Geography in the Middle Ages*, Chap. 8; A. P. Newton, ed., *Travel and Travellers of the Middle Ages* (London: Routledge, 1926), Chap. 10, "The Search for the Sea Route to India," by E. Prestage.

11 See, for example, the discussion on hoards of Roman gold coins in southern India by Sir Mortimer Wheeler in his *Rome Beyond the Imperial Frontiers* (London: Pelican Books, 1955), Chap. 12.

12 A stimulating recent interpretation of Portuguese history in the thirteenth, fourteenth, and fifteenth centuries is to be found in Chaps. 4–8 of J. B. Trend, *Portugal* (London: Benn, 1957).

13 On the subject of Castilian ventures to West Africa in the fifteenth century, see J. W. Blake, *Europeans in West Africa, 1450–1560* ("Hakluyt Society, 2nd Series," Nos. 86 and 87 [2 vols.; London: 1942]), I, 185–246; also his *European Beginnings in West Africa, 1454–1578* (London: Longmans, 1937), Chaps. 1–4.

14 Among these was Jaffuda Cresques, son of the Abraham Cresques of Majorca who had been responsible for the Catalan Atlas of 1375.

15 On Henry the Navigator, see R. H. Major, *Life of Prince Henry the Navigator* (London: 1868), and J. P. Oliveira Martins, *The Golden Age of Prince Henry the Navigator*, English trans. by J. J. Abraham, and W. E. Reynolds (London: Chapman and

Hall, 1914). For a more recent general study, see Edgar Prestage, *The Portuguese Pioneers* (London: Black, 1933).

16 Gomes Eannes de Azurara, *The Chronicle of the Discovery and Conquest of Guinea,* trans. and ed. by C. R. Beazley, and E. Prestage ("Hakluyt Society, 1st Series," Nos. 95 and 100 [London: 1896 and 1898]). An abridged translation which is still in print is *The Conquests and Discoveries of Henry the Navigator,* ed. V. De Castro e Almeida and trans. by Bernard Miall (London: Allen & Unwin, 1936).

17 This point can be illustrated by the eagerness with which the Portuguese were willing, as late as *c.* 1486, to interpret the information which they gathered at Benin about a powerful monarch of the hinterland, the Ogane, in terms of a Christian monarch to be identified with Prester John. The Ogane was almost certainly the Oni of Ife, who is still called the Oghene by the people of Benin. By this time it was known in Portugal that "Prester John" was located "in the land above Egypt whence it stretched to the southern sea" (Abyssinian envoys had visited Spain as early as 1427 and Lisbon in 1452); the Portuguese simply had no idea of the breadth of Africa (Ife is about 100 miles from Benin, Abyssinia some 2,000 miles). See João de Barros's *Asia* (1552), Decade I, Bk. III, Chap. 4, in G. R. Crone, *The Voyages of Cadamosto and Other Documents* ("Hakluyt Society, 2nd Series, No. 80 [London: 1937]), pp. 126–28, and also R. E. Bradbury, *The Benin Kingdom* ("International African Institute; Ethnographic Survey, Western Africa," Part XIII [London: 1957]), p. 20.

18 In the long run probably the most important discovery was that of the rich fishing banks of the Mauretanian coast.

19 Bovill, *Golden Trade of the Moors,* p. 119, n. 1.

20 Jean Léon l'Africain, *Description de l'Afrique,* II, p. 464 and n. 22.

21 Maurice Delafosse, *Haut-Sénégal-Niger* (3 vols.; Paris: Larose, 1912), III, 277.

22 I use the translation of Bernard Miall, *Conquests and Discoveries of Henry the Navigator,* p. 196. The actual Portuguese words are "E esta gente desta terra verde, é tôda negra, e porem é chamada terra dos Negros, ou terra de Guinee, por cujo aazo os homeẽs e molheres della som chamados Guineus, que quer tanto dizer como negros."

23 Seventeen and a half Portuguese leagues are usually reckoned to the degree; 100 leagues was thus equivalent to some 340 nautical miles.

24   On Gomes and his activities see Barros's *Asia,* Dec. I, Bk. II, Chap. 2, in Crone, *Voyages of Cadamosto,* pp. 107–14, and comment in Blake, *Europeans in West Africa,* I, 4–18.

25   Recent work by modern French authorities, notably De la Roncière, *La découverte de l'Afrique au moyen âge,* II, Chap. 2, and Raymond Mauny, "Les prétendues navigations dieppoises a la Côte occidentale d'Afrique au XIVᵉ siècle," *Bulletin de l'Institut Française d'Afrique Noire,* XII, No. 1 (Jan., 1950), 122–34, would seem finally to have disposed of the idea, originating principally with Villault de Bellefond in 1669, that Normans from Dieppe reached Cape Verde in 1364 and were established on the Gold Coast *c.* 1380–*c.* 1410. There is an extensive collection of references to this subject in Yusuf Kamal, *Monumenta Cartographica,* IV (Cairo: 1937), fasc. 2, 1271–74. It is possible that the traditions of a French post at Elmina recorded by Eva L. R. Meyerowitz, *Akan Traditions of Origin* (London: Faber, 1952), pp. 70–72, relate not to the fourteenth century, but to a brief French occupation in 1582.

26   *Conquests and Discoveries of Henry the Navigator,* p. 152.

27   Considerable efforts were in fact made to intercept or to divert the flow of gold from Wangara. A fort was built at Arguin, an island in the lee of Cape Blanco, *c.* 1448 and for some years at the close of the fifteenth century, a post was maintained inland at Wadan, some 250 miles east of Arguin, in an attempt to intercept the caravan route running north from Walata. Further south, the Portuguese tried to penetrate inland up the Senegal and Gambia rivers directly towards Wangara, and even sent embassies to Mali and Timbuctu. See Blake, *Europeans in West Africa,* I, 22–25, 33–35.

28   Barros, *Asia,* Dec. I, Bk. II, Chap. 2, in Crone, *Voyages of Cadamosto,* pp. 109–10.

29   Reasonably accurate accounts of African gold mining in the Gold Coast are rare before the nineteenth century, since it was not until then that Europeans ventured far from the coast. There is a description based on hearsay in Pieter de Marees, *A Description and Historical Declaration of the Golden Kingdom of Guinea* (1602) in *Purchas His Pilgrims* (Glasgow: Maclehose, 1905), VI, 347–48; and a longer and better account in William Bosman, *A New and Accurate Description of the Coast of Guinea* (London: 1705), Letter VI, pp. 80–81. For a modern account, see R. F. Burton and V. L. Cameron, *To the Gold Coast for Gold* (London: 1883), II, especially pp. 112–13, 160–61, 174–75, 219, 294.

30   See above, p. 20.
31   Blake, *Europeans in West Africa*, I, 97–98, and 76, n. 1; Duarte Pacheco Pereira, *Esmeraldo de Situ Orbis* [*c.* 1505–8], trans. and ed. G. H. T. Kimble ("Hakluyt Society, 2nd Series," No. 79 [London: 1936]), pp. 117, 120.
32   This can only be the roughest of estimates. From figures given in Blake, *Europeans in West Africa*, I, 92–93, 107, and by Pacheco Pereira, *Esmeraldo*, pp. 117, 120, it might seem as though *c.* 1500, the gold obtained from Mina amounted to about 24,000 ozs. a year, say £ 100,000. This would seem a maximum figure. Total world gold production at this time has been estimated at rather less than £ 1,000,000.
33   Ruy de Pina (1440–1521) succeeded Azurara (died *c.* 1473) as royal chronicler.
34   In Blake, *Europeans in West Africa*, I, 70.
35   De Marees, *Description . . . of Guinea* in *Purchas*, VI, 304. This abridged translation is the only one in English. The full Dutch version is available in a modern edition by S. P. l'Honoré Naber "Linschoten Vereeniging," V [The Hague: 1912]), pp. 88, 211–12. A French translation was published at Amsterdam in 1605.
36   There is a well illustrated modern discussion of the Gold Coast castles in W. J. Varley, "The Forts and Castles of the Gold Coast," *TGCTHS*, I, Part 1 (1952). It is now known, however, that the whole of the basic structure of Elmina is of Portuguese origin, though much of the original stone work was later faced with Dutch brick.
37   See C. R. Boxer, *The Dutch in Brazil, 1624–1654* (Oxford: Clarendon Press, 1957), p. 84 and also pp. 5–6.
38   Blake, *Europeans in West Africa,* I, 59–63.
39   Boxer, *Dutch in Brazil,* pp. 17–33, and also 140–44.
40   See Blake, *Europeans in West Africa,* I, 59–60. The demand for imported slaves on the Gold Coast was probably occasioned by the fact that the exports of the country brought to the coast by merchants from the interior tended to be of small bulk in proportion to their value (e.g., gold), while the European imports received in exchange (e.g., cloth) were of relatively great bulk, and slaves were required for their transport into the hinterland.
41   See C. R. Boxer, *Salvador de Sá and the Struggle for Brazil and Angola* (London: Athlone Press, 1952).
42   Accurate statistics of the Atlantic slave trade do not exist before the nineteenth century, when of course the trade was under the abolitionist searchlight. However, the independent estimates

made by the demographer R. R. Kucynski, *Population Move-*
ments (London: Oxford University Press, 1936), pp. 8–17, and
the historian Reginald Coupland, *The British Anti-Slavery Move-*
ment (London: Home University Library, 1933), Chap. 1,
based mainly on the figures available for imports at some American ports for some periods, agree remarkably well. It should
be remembered that the estimates are for slaves *landed in*
America; allowing for losses en route, the figures for slaves
leaving Africa must be higher, possibly by 20%. There is a
useful account of the trade at the end of the eighteenth century
in Bryan Edwards, *The History, Civil and Commercial, of the*
British Colonies in the West Indies (4th ed., 3 vols.; London:
1807), II, 58–147.

43   One of the best, certainly one of the best known, accounts of
the eighteenth century Gold Coast and its forts is that of
William Bosman, a factor in the Dutch West India Company,
in his *A New and Accurate Description of the Coast of Guinea,*
first published in English in 1705 and reprinted in facsimile
for Sir Alfred Jones of Elder, Dempster and Co., Liverpool, in
1907. See also John Barbot, *A Description of the Coasts of North*
and South Guinea in *Churchill's Voyages* (London: 1732), Vol.
V; and William Smith, *Thirty Different Draughts of Guinea*
(London: *c.* 1728), and his *A New Voyage to Guinea* (London:
1744).

44   This figure of £200,000 is based on Bosman, *New and Accurate*
Description, p. 89, where he estimates the total exports in a
good year at 7000 marks, taking a mark to be 8 ozs. and an
ounce to be worth £4. Bosman put the English share of the
trade at 2200 marks, of which the Royal African Company,
which officially held a monopoly of the English trade, took 1200
marks, i.e., roughly £38,000. This would seem high in relation
to the figure of £250,000 recorded as the total of gold imports
by the Company during the eleven years 1682–92; see K. G.
Davies, *The Royal African Company* (London: Longmans,
1957), p. 225. But as Davies says, the gold trade was subject
to considerable fluctuations in volume (due to internal wars),
and Bosman's over-all estimate is for *a good year.*

45   See, for example, Edwards, *History . . . of the . . . West*
Indies, II, 65–67.

46   See Bosman's remark, *New and Accurate Description,* p. 330,
about Keta: "Their trade is that of slaves." Almost all Bosman's
remarks about the slave trade refer to the Slave Coast, not to
the Gold Coast.

47   For example, Bosman's figures, *ibid.*, p. 89, for the gold trade on the Gold Coast suggest that the external trade of the Gold Coast was divided roughly as follows *c.* 1700: English 31%, Dutch 43%, other Europeans 26%. Bryan Edwards's figures, *History . . . West Indies*, II, 65–67, for the slave trade suggest that it was divided *c.* 1770–85 roughly as follows: on the Gold Coast, British traders 75%; in West Africa as a whole, British 52%, French 27%, Dutch 5%, others 16%.

48   See Barros, *Asia*, Dec. I, Bk. III, Chap. 2, in Crone, *Voyages of Cadamosto*, pp. 122–23; also, comment in Blake, *Europeans in West Africa*, I, 41–43.

49   On the "Notes" in particular, and relations between the Europeans of the forts and the Africans in general, see Blake, *Europeans in West Africa*, I, 43–57, and Hon. H. A. Wyndham, *The Atlantic and Slavery* (London: Oxford University Press, 1935), pp. 8–33.

50   After *c.* 1750, the garrisons and armament of the English forts were allowed to deteriorate to a dangerous degree. See, for example, *Report from the Committee on African Forts* (1815–17), Parliamentary Papers, 1817, VI (431), pp. 7–8, and 1816, VII (506), pp. 135, 183, 184, 190, 191.

51   For example, the destruction of the Portuguese fort at Accra already mentioned; the occupation of the British fort at Winneba by Agona in 1663 and in 1679; the occupation of the Danish fort Christiansborg by Akwamu during 1693–94; and the occupation of the Dutch fort at Kormantin by an Ashanti army in 1807.

52   On the situation in the coastal settlements, see Wyndham, *The Atlantic and Slavery*, pp. 8–33.

53   On the Slave Coast, see *ibid.*, pp. 34–43. The conflicts in the Niger delta in the nineteenth century have been analysed by K. Onwuka Dike, *Trade and Politics in the Niger Delta, 1830–1855* (Oxford: Clarendon Press, 1956).

It should be remarked that the geology of the Gold Coast between Akim and Accra provided better conditions for the erection of coastal forts than are to be found further to the east. A series of rocky ridges jut seawards as small promontories, affording good building material and, on their eastern lees, sheltered landing places. East of Accra (and also west of Axim), the coast is generally low, sandy, and unindented.

54   It is around Little Popo, the modern Anecho, that the Gẽ people are to be found. See p. 24.

55   The Danes had earlier joined with the people of Osu (where Christiansborg is situated) to repulse an Akwamu attack.

56 In 1660, the Swedish fort (the modern Christiansborg) passed into Dutch hands. It was then successively in Danish, Portuguese, Danish, and Akwamu occupation until 1694, when the Danes secured it permanently.

57 Bosman, *A New and Accurate Description,* p. 78.

58 This account and interpretation of Akwamu history is based on an article by Ivor Wilks in *THSG,* III, Part 2, 1957 (1958). See also W. E. F. Ward, *A History of the Gold Coast* (London: Allen & Unwin, 1948), pp. 97–107.

59 Ward, *Gold Coast,* p. 49, n. 1. See also n. 60 below.

60 The central (i.e., Kumasi) tradition of Ashanti is set down in Sir Francis Fuller, *A Vanished Dynasty, Ashanti* (London: Murray, 1921). See also Ward, *Gold Coast,* pp. 107–19, 130–54. The fundamental authority on Ashanti is R. S. Rattray, and is likely to remain so for many years. See his (1) *Ashanti,* 1923 (reprinted 1955), (2) *Religion and Art in Ashanti,* 1927 (reprinted 1954), (3) *Ashanti Law and Constitution,* 1929 (reprinted 1956), all London: Oxford University Press. See in particular (3), Chap. 24 on Okomfo Anokye; (1), Chap. 23 on the Golden Stool, and pp. 95–98, 297–98 on stools generally.

61 That is, following European embassies to Kumasi. See in particular T. E. Bowditch, *Mission from Cape Coast Castle to Ashantee* (London: 1819), and Joseph Dupuis, *Journal of a Residence in Ashantee* (London: H. Colburn, 1824), both of whom provide excellent descriptions and accounts of Ashanti history.

62 The first of the Notes to come into Ashanti hands would seem to be that for Elmina. The Edina state having become tributary to Denkyera, the Note passed to Ashanti after the defeat of Denkyera.

Chapter III

1 W. W. Claridge, *A History of the Gold Coast and Ashanti* (2 vols; London: Murray, 1915); W. E. F. Ward, *A History of the Gold Coast* (London: Allen & Unwin, 1948). Although Mr. Ward gives much more attention to early tradition and to modern economic and social history than does Claridge, approximately half of his book is still essentially concerned with the political history of the years from 1816 to 1902.

2 In the last resort, the American demand for slaves was bound to continue as long as slavery existed on the American continent. Although the victory of the North in the Civil War ensured the extinction of slavery in the United States, the legal status of

slavery was not finally abolished in Cuba until 1886 and in Brazil until 1888. A self-styled Brazilian slave trader, one Geraldo da Lima, remained active in the Ewe country just east of the Volta until well on in the 1860's.—Ward, *Gold Coast,* pp. 219–21, also pp. 309–11.

3   See Ward, *Gold Coast,* pp. 231–33.

4   Geraldo da Lima (see n. 2 above), for example, was in league with the people of the Anlo state, which was an ally of Ashanti in the campaigns of 1863–74. Anlo is on the coast just east of the Volta, and one of the most active and successful Ashanti armies was operating to the east of the river during 1866–70.

5   Nevertheless, politics and business did not always see eye to eye. It is reported that in the two years previous to the British expedition against Ashanti in 1873, the British firm of F. & A. Swanzy, one of the most successful houses established on the Gold Coast, sent 18,139 muskets and 29,062 kegs of gunpowder to Ashanti, mainly through Half Assini, a village in the extreme west of the Gold Coast.—Henry Swanzy, "A Trading Family in the Nineteenth Century Gold Coast," *TGCTHS,* II, Part 2 (1956), 115.

6   On the naval and diplomatic action of Britain against the Atlantic slave trade, see Christopher Lloyd, *The Navy and the Slave Trade* (London: Longmans, 1949), especially Chaps. 4–9; also R. Coupland, *The British Anti-Slavery Movement* (London: Home University Library, 1933), Chap. 6.

7   The most outstanding exposition of these positive principles in relation to West Africa was Sir T. Fowell Buxton's *The African Slave Trade and Its Remedy* (London: 1839; 2nd ed., 1840). See also J. Gallagher, "Fowell Buxton and the New African Policy, 1838–42," *Cambridge Historical Journal,* XI (1950), 36–58. But the seeds of the positive policy can be seen as far back as Wilberforce's speeches urging the abolition of the British slave trade.

8   There is no substantial study of missionary activity and its effects on the Gold Coast. A general outline can be found in the various volumes of C. P. Groves, *The Planting of Christianity in Africa* (4 vols.; London: Lutterworth Press, 1948–57). Greater detail can be gleaned only from the annual reports and the histories of the various missionary societies, of which the Wesleyan Methodist Missionary Society and the Basel Mission are the most significant, and from accounts of individual missions and missionaries: see, for example, A. E. Southon, *Gold Coast Methodism* (London: Cargate Press, and Cape Coast: Methodist Book

Depot, 1934); F. D. Walker, *Thomas Birch Freeman* (London: Student Christian Movement Press, and Cape Coast: Methodist Book Depot, 1929); Dennis Kemp, *Nine Years at the Gold Coast* (London: Macmillan, 1898).

9 It must not be forgotten that the processes of Europeanisation and Christianisation had in fact begun before the missionary onslaught, and that in fact the way of the latter had been prepared by the activities of the traders. Thus, for example, the first schools on the Gold Coast were those run by the chaplains in the forts for the children of the forts' staff and hangers-on. See, for example, the account of the life of Philip Quaque, 1741–1816, the first African chaplain at Cape Coast Castle, by F. L. Bartels in *TGCTHS*, I, Part 5 (1955), 153–77, and the article "Notable Danish Chaplains on the Gold Coast" by H. Debrunner in *TGCTHS*, II, Part 1 (1956), 13–30. It was the desire of African ex-pupils of the school at Cape Coast Castle for Bibles and for further Christian instruction, which led to the establishment of the Wesleyan Methodist mission on the Gold Coast from 1834 onwards.

10 Among notable early examples of this new elite may be instanced James Bannerman, the mulatto merchant who acted as governor of the British Gold Coast settlements in 1850–51; G. K. Blankson, a merchant and J.P., who in 1861 became the first full-blooded African member of the British Legislative Council; J. M. Sarbah, who, in 1887, was the first native of the Gold Coast to be called to the English Bar; Hendrik Vroom, one of the first District Commissioners of the British colony which was proclaimed in 1874, who was later awarded the C.M.G.; Rev. C. C. Reindorf, pastor of the Basel Mission and author of *The History of the Gold Coast and Asante* (Basel: 1895); G. E. Ferguson, a surveyor and an early British agent in the Northern Territories; Dr. G. W. Quartey-Papafio, appointed a government medical officer in 1888; and, of course, the men concerned with the Fante Confederation and later with the Aborigines' Rights Protection Society. Magnus Sampson's *Gold Coast Men of Affairs* (London: Stockwell, 1937) is a work of homage to men such as these. For a more dispassionate study, we must await David Kimble's forthcoming *Political History of the Gold Coast, 1850–1928* (Oxford University Press).

11 See J. D. Fage, "The Administration of George Maclean on the Gold Coast, 1830–44," *TGCTHS*, I, Part 4 (1955), 115–16.

12 The subject of Dutch relations with the Gold Coast in the nineteenth century is currently being studied by Dr. Douglas

Coombs of the University College of Ghana. Something is said on this point in his article, "The Place of the 'Certificate of Apologie' in Ghanaian History," in *THSG*, III, Part 3, 1958 (1959).

13 At the close of the eighteenth century and in the early years of the nineteenth, there were a number of Danish attempts to establish plantations on the eastern Gold Coast. See C. D. Adams, "Activities of Danish Botanists in Guinea, 1783–1850," *THSG*, III, Part 1 (1957), 30–46.

14 On this subject, see B. E. Kwaw-Swanzy, "Constitutional Development of the Gold Coast, 1901–25" (Unpublished M. Litt. thesis, Cambridge University, 1955), Chap. 2.

15 Between 1880 and 1904, 476 companies, with a nominal capital totalling nearly £43,000,000, were registered for gold mining and mining exploration in West Africa, the bulk of these expecting to operate in the Gold Coast. But in 1904, there were only four companies in the Gold Coast with outputs of gold worth more than £10,000.—S. H. Frankel, *Capital Investment in Africa* (London: Oxford University Press, 1938), pp. 162–63. An entertaining view of the boom is provided in R. F. Burton and V. L. Cameron, *To the Gold Coast for Gold* (London: 1883).

16 The Orders in Council were signed on September 26, 1901, but did not come into operation until January 1, 1902.

17 There had in fact been an abortive education ordinance as early as 1852. See Colin G. Wise, *A History of Education in British West Africa* (London: Longmans, 1956), p. 31. The 1882 ordinance was a standard one adopted by all the British West African territories.

18 The increasing share of government in the field of education may be simply illustrated by a few figures. In 1880–81, there were some 139 schools in the Gold Coast. Two of these were government schools costing between £800 and £900 a year. The others were mission schools receiving a grand total of £425 a year in government grants. By 1902, government was running seven schools itself and provided grants totalling £3,875 to 117 mission schools: expenditure on education amounted to 1.75% of a total government expenditure of some £523,000. In 1950, on the eve of the rapid advances which led to self-government in 1957, of 2,904 primary schools, 41 were directly run by government and 1,551 received government grants; and of 56 secondary schools, 12 were financially assisted by government. There were also 19 teacher-training colleges, all in receipt of government aid, and the University College, also substantially

financed by government. Ten per cent of a total government recurrent expenditure of £12,232,000 was on education. See J. H. Nketia, "Progress in Gold Coast Education," *TGCTHS*, I, Part 3 (1954), pp. 1–9, for a short summary; also F. H. Hilliard, *A Short History of Education in British West Africa* (London: Nelson, 1957), pp. 69–117, and Wise, *History of Education in British West Africa*.

19 See H. J. Bevin, "The Gold Coast Economy about 1880," *TGCTHS*, II, Part 2 (1956), 72–86.

20 Statistics of Gold Coast trade and finance for the years 1900–1936 are conveniently set out in Tables 78–79 of Frankel's *Capital Investment in Africa*, of which pp. 316–25 deal with the Gold Coast. For years after 1936, the most accessible sources are probably the annual series of *Colonial Reports: Gold Coast* (London: H.M.S.O.).

21 There seems no reason to doubt the well-established tradition that a Gold Coast native named Tetteh Quashie, who had been a labourer on the plantations of the Portuguese island of Fernando Po, one of the principal sources of supply of cocoa before the rise of Gold Coast cocoa production, brought back cocoa with him on his return in 1879. On the other hand it seems that cocoa seedlings were being cultivated at Akropong by the Basel Mission in the 1860's. The first introduction of cocoa may have been even earlier, but interpretation of the earlier sources is made difficult by confusion between "cocoa" (for "cacao") and "coco" (the nut). The Basel Mission and government botanical gardens undoubtedly played an important role in propagating and distributing seedlings, but Tetteh Quashie, from his Fernando Po experience, may well have been the first African to appreciate the value of the plant to the Gold Coast farmer, and one of the first to demonstrate that it would thrive under local farming methods.

22 The best modern study is Polly Hill, *The Gold Coast Cocoa Farmer: A Preliminary Survey* (London: Oxford University Press, 1956). From her extensive firsthand knowledge, the author is very chary of generalising about the size of farms.

23 Frankel, *Capital Investment in Africa*, pp. 320–24.

24 *Colonial Reports: Gold Coast, 1950* (London: H.M.S.O., 1952), p. 15. During the cocoa season 1949–50, the average selling price of Gold Coast cocoa in London was £178 per ton. Since 1950, prices have been even higher as the following seasonal averages show: 1950–51, £268; 1951–52, £245; 1952–53, £231; 1953–54, £359; 1954–55, £355.—Annual *Reports of*

Cocoa Marketing Board (Accra), for years ending on September 30. The effects of swollen shoot have also been in part offset by new plantings in areas little affected by the disease, which has been most dangerous in the areas where cocoa has been cultivated longest. Thus whereas in 1936–37, the eastern Gold Coast produced 43% of the crop and Ashanti only 30%, in 1949–50, Ashanti produced 47% and the eastern Gold Coast only 27%.

25   On this subject see Thomas Hodgkin, *Nationalism in Colonial Africa* (London: Muller, 1956), Part II, Chap. 2 *et seq.*

26   The nature of the problems resulting, particularly in the new towns, from the breakdown of the traditional social relationships and their inherent social security can be seen in K. A. Busia, *A Social Survey of Sekondi-Takoradi* (London: Crown Agents for the Colonies, 1950).

27   *Gold Coast Revenue* (£ 1000)

	Total Revenue	Total Customs Revenue	% of Customs to Total Revenue	Yield of Cocoa Export Duty
1900	333	281	84.4	—
1913	1,302	780	59.9	—
1928	3,914	2,603	66.5	263
1951	30,764	21,431	69.7	10,766

Sources: Frankel, *Capital Investment,* p. 322, Table 79; *Colonial Reports: Gold Coast: 1952* (1953), pp. 17, 126.

28   The Cocoa Marketing Board emerged out of an over-all system of produce marketing developed during World War II, when the whole of the cocoa crop was purchased by the British government. See F. M. Bourret, *The Gold Coast: A Survey of the Gold Coast and British Togoland, 1919–46* (Palo Alto: Stanford University Press, 1949), pp. 176–78. In 1949 an Agricultural Produce Marketing Board was set up to perform similar services for other export crops. The ideology and policy of the marketing boards are very critically examined by P. T. Bauer in his *West African Trade* (Cambridge University Press, 1954).

29   In 1954, the export duty on cocoa was determined in such a way that, when the world price was £ 260 or more per ton f.o.b. Gold Coast, the Cocoa Marketing Board would not receive more than £ 180 per ton. In 1954–55, the average price secured for Gold Coast cocoa was £ 355 per ton, which was divided as follows:

£175 export duty to Gold Coast government,
£18 buying and other expenses of C.M.B.,
£135 to the farmer,
£27 surplus, to C.M.B. reserves.

For the following season, the price paid to the farmer was raised to £149 per ton.

By 30 September 1955, the gross surpluses of the C.M.B. had amounted to £89,921,689, and among the purposes for which it had given or lent funds since 1947 were the rehabilitation of swollen shoot areas (£9,400,000), harbour and railway expansion (£11,293,000), the University College of the Gold Coast (£2,000,000), educational scholarships (£3,000,000), and rural development (£1,178,000).—Annual *Reports of Cocoa Marketing Board*.

30 In the half century from 1851 to 1900, fifteen individuals held the substantive post of governor, eight of whom had more than one tour of duty on the coast. During the same period, nineteen individuals had appreciable periods, in between substantive appointments or while the governor was absent on leave, as acting governor. In all, 34 different persons had charge of British affairs on the Gold Coast during this fifty-year period (three acting governors later became substantive governors). The only periods of reasonable continuity were 1867–72, when H. T. Ussher had three successive tours of duty as governor, and after 1886, when Sir W. Brandford Griffith was governor for five successive tours 1886–95, being succeeded first by Sir W. E. Maxwell (two tours, 1895–97), and then by Sir F. M. Hodgson (two tours, 1898–1900), who had already acted as governor whenever, during 1889–98, Griffith and Maxwell had been absent.

31 The Gold Coast came under the governor of Sierra Leone during 1821–28, was under the merchants 1828–43, came under Sierra Leone again during 1844–50, was an independent colony during 1850–66, came under Sierra Leone for the third time during 1866–74, and finally became an independent colony in 1874, though until 1886 its governor was also responsible for the colony of Lagos.

32 For an account and estimation of Maclean's work on the Gold Coast, see Fage, "Administration of George Maclean," *TGCTHS*, I, Part 4, 104–20. A full-length biographical study by Mr. G. E. Metcalfe is shortly to be published by Oxford University Press.

33 Ironically enough one of the criticisms of Maclean's regime was that he did not take active steps against foreign slave-trading

ships putting in to the landing places under his control, on the grounds that they were not within his jurisdiction.

34 Parliamentary Papers, 1842, XI (551), Part I, p. 5.

35 Hill had previously been one of the most active officers in the West African squadron of the Royal Navy which was engaged in anti-slave trade patrols.

36 6 Victoria c. 13, and 6 and 7 Victoria c. 94.

37 For a description of the role of the Judicial Assessor, see W. R. Bronlow, *Memoir of Sir James Marshall* (London: Burns & Oates, 1890). Marshall was appointed Judicial Assessor in 1873.

38 *Collection of Treaties with Native Chiefs, etc. of the West Coast of Africa*, Part III, Gold Coast, No. 4.

39 On this point, and on the nature and significance of the Bond itself, see the article by Dr. J. B. Danquah, himself an outstanding nationalist leader of the 1940's, "The Historical Significance of the Bond of 1844," *THSG*, III, Part 1 (1957), 1–29.

40 For an examination of this period, see G. E. Metcalfe, "After Maclean: Some Aspects of British Gold Coast Policy in the Mid-nineteenth Centurty," *TGCTHS*, I, Part 5 (1955), 178–92.

41 Parliamentary Papers, 1865, V (412), *Report from Select Committee on the West African Settlements*. This enquiry, like that of 1842, covered all the British settlements in West Africa, and not merely the Gold Coast. See also J. J. Crooks, *Records of the Gold Coast Settlements, 1750–1874* (Dublin: Browne & Nolan, 1923), pp. 369–70, which gives a useful selection of extracts from the parliamentary papers and other official documents of the period.

42 The origins of the movement which became the Fante Confederation lie in the alliance of some of the Fante states in 1868 to support the people of the state of Kommenda in their opposition to the transfer of the British fort there to the Dutch. —See p. 60. Since the centre of Dutch influence was at Elmina, and Elmina was traditionally associated with Ashanti (see Chap. II, n. 62), this Fante alliance was fundamentally opposed not only to the Dutch, but also to Ashanti, whose armies had been campaigning towards the south since 1863. In view of the passive attitude of the British towards Gold Coast problems in general, and the Ashanti threat in particular, it was not unnatural that the alliance should develop into a permanent political association to take over from the British. The complicated political background of the years 1863–74 is ably set

out, and the Fante Confederation is sympathetically viewed, in Ward, *Gold Coast,* pp. 225–60. The text of the constitution of the Confederation may be found in J. E. Casely Hayford, *Gold Coast Native Institutions* (London: Sweet & Maxwell, 1903), pp. 327–40.

43 See above, p. 64.

44 The formal position had been quite clear to the 1842 Select Committee when it reported: "It is to be remembered that our compulsory authority is strictly limited . . . by our title . . . to the British forts, and that the magistrates [of the forts] are strictly prohibited from exercising jurisdiction even over the natives and districts immediately under the influence and protection of the forts. All jurisdiction over the natives beyond the forts must, therefore, be considered as optional, and should be made the subject of distinct agreement, as to its nature and limits, with the native chiefs. . . . Their relation to the English Crown should be, not the allegiance of subjects, to which we have no right to pretend, and which it would entail an inconvenient responsibility to possess, but the deference of weaker powers to a stronger and more enlightened neighbour, whose protection and counsel they seek, and to whom they are bound by certain definite obligations."—Crooks, *Records,* p. 280. But one effect of the Bond, occasioned by the scruples of the 1842 Committee, had been to incline the British officials to act more and more as an administration for the coastal states, and so to assume that their people did owe allegiance to the British Crown, even though the home authorities in 1865 had shown themselves only too aware of the "inconveniences" involved in such an allegiance.

45 Mr. David Kimble has kindly allowed me to see the MS of his forthcoming *Political History of the Gold Coast,* in which Chap. 14 is entitled "Education and African Leadership." From this it appears, *inter alia,* that in 1883 there were 43 senior posts in the administration, of which 9 were then held by Gold Coast Africans. In addition, the Colonial Postmaster was a Sierra Leonean. By 1908, there were 274 senior appointments, only 5 of which were held by Africans. In 1919, the year of Guggisberg's arrival, only 2 Africans held senior posts, one of them on a temporary basis. By 1926, the position was 28 African compared with 481 European appointments. The problem is also discussed in pp. 156–83 of Heather Dalton, "The Development of the Gold Coast under British Administration, 1874–1901" (Unpublished M.A. thesis, University of London, 1957). On

the more general point about the development of the British Colonial Service, see Martin Wight, *The Development of the Legislative Council 1606–1945* (London: Faber, 1946), pp. 54–55 and also Sir Charles Jefferies, *The Colonial Empire and Its Civil Service* (Cambridge University Press, 1938).

46   There were in fact two bills, the first being the Crown Lands Bill of 1894, which was eventually replaced by the Public Lands Bill of 1897.

47   There is an outline of the lands controversy in Ward, *Gold Coast*, pp. 329–35; see also Kimble's forthcoming *Political History of the Gold Coast*, Chaps. 5 and 8.

48   On the political programme of the Gold Coast Aborigines' Rights Protection Society, see Kwaw-Swanzy, *Constitutional Development of the Gold Coast*, Chap. 10, and Kimble, *Political History*, Chap. 5.

49   For an examination of the institution of the Legislative Council in the British Crown Colonies generally, including a comparison with the colonial Assemblies of the old empire before 1783, see Wight, *Development of the Legislative Council;* for the Legislative Council in the Gold Coast, see the same author's *Gold Coast Legislative Council* (London: Faber, 1947).

50   It is an open question whether in fact the Legislative Council of a British Crown Colony can evolve naturally into a sovereign parliament. If a distinctive feature of the Legislative Council of a Crown Colony is that "it can contain not only nominated unofficial members . . . but also elected members" (Wight, *Development of the Legislative Council*, p. 72), it is also true that "the official majority is the characteristic institution of crown colony government."—*ibid.*, p. 100. The character of a Legislative Council is very different from that of the British Parliament; it is government meeting to do the business it wants done and has planned, in the view of representatives of the governed and as far as possible with their consent. The initiative lies always with the officials who are responsible only to the governor. See also Wight, *Gold Coast Legislative Council*, p. 77.

51   See Decima Moore [Lady Guggisberg], *We Two in West Africa* (London: Heinemann, 1909).

52   It is now evident that, particularly in the political sphere, many of Guggisberg's policies had been anticipated by Clifford. This is stressed by Kwaw-Swanzy, *Constitutional Development of the Gold Coast;* see especially Chap. 7, pp. 185–95; Chap. 10, pp. 277–79, 288–89. Lady Clifford edited *Our Days on the Gold Coast* (London: J. Murray, 1919).

53   Aggrey, a native of the Gold Coast, was a very remarkable man.

See Edwin W. Smith, *Aggrey of Africa* (London: Student Christian Movement Press, 1929), which is also valuable for Fraser and for the conception of Achimota. Guggisberg's views on education can be seen in his *The Keystone* (London: Simpkin, 1924); see also Sir Gordon Guggisberg, and A. G. Fraser, *The Future of the Negro* (London: Student Christian Movement Press, 1929).

54 A definitive study of Guggisberg and his times is still to come. In the meantime reference may be made to F. M. Bourret's useful *The Gold Coast: A Survey*, Chaps. 3 and 4 of which are wholly devoted to Guggisberg and his work. There is also a great deal of value on Guggisberg's political programme in Wight, *Gold Coast Legislative Council*. See also the article on Guggisberg by Lord Olivier in *Dictionary of National Biography, 1922–1930* (London: 1937). Guggisberg's own views and his estimation of his achievements can be seen best in his lengthy addresses to Legislative Council on the occasion of the annual estimates sessions. These were separately printed; of particular value is the 1927 address, *The Gold Coast: A Review of the Events of 1920–1926 and the Prospects of 1927–1928* (Accra: Govt. Printer, 1927).

55 Until 1946, the competence of the Legislative Council was limited to the Gold Coast Colony in the narrow sense; the governor was the sole legislator for Ashanti and for the Northern Territories Protectorate. Consequently until 1946, only the Colony had representation in the Council. See, *inter alia*, Wight, *Gold Coast Legislative Council*, pp. 191–96. However, Guggisberg's care for coöperation with the traditional authorities in Ashanti is shown by his sponsorship of Capt. R. S. Rattray's anthropological researches which paved the way for the restoration of the Ashanti Confederacy Council in 1936.

56 The published works of Sarbah and Casely Hayford throw an interesting light on Gold Coast nationalism in the period *c.* 1890 to *c.* 1920, viz. John Mensah Sarbah, *Fanti Customary Laws* (1897); *Fanti Law Reports* (1904); *Fanti National Constitution* (1906), all London: Clowes; J. E. Casely Hayford, *Gold Coast Native Institutions; The Truth about the West African Land Question* (London: Phillips, 1904 and 1913); *Ethiopia Unbound* (London: Phillips, 1911). See also *West African Leadership: Public Speeches . . . by Casely Hayford*, ed. Magnus J. Sampson (Ilfracombe: Stockwell, 1949); and J. W. De Graft Johnson, *Towards Nationhood in West Africa* (London: Headley, 1928).

57 The programme of the National Congress also included the

establishment of West African universities and the appointment of Africans as judges. The University College of the Gold Coast (now University College of Ghana) was in fact founded in 1948. There had been an African judge, Frans Smith, during 1887–1908; the next, Sir Leslie M'Carthy, was not appointed until 1940.

58 This new approach, of which the Colonial Development and Welfare Act passed by the British Parliament in 1945 was symptomatic, was most cogently argued in a short book published by Professor W. K. Hancock during the war, *Argument of Empire* (London: Penguin Books, 1943).

59 This was the first legislature to include representatives from Ashanti as well as the coastal Colony; the representation of the Northern Territories did not come until 1951. The total composition of the 1946 Legislative Council was, besides the Governor, six official members (Europeans), six nominated unofficial members (European or African), and eighteen directly or indirectly elected African members. See Wight, *Gold Coast Legislative Council*, Appendices 2, 4, and 5.

60 *Report of the Commission of Enquiry into Disturbances in the Gold Coast, 1948* [Watson Report], Colonial No. 231 (London: H.M.S.O., 1948). See paras. 97–122, especially para. 101.

61 *Gold Coast: Report to His Excellency the Governor by the Committee on Constitutional Reform, 1949* [Coussey Report], Colonial No. 248 (London: H.M.S.O., 1949). Coussey was subsequently knighted.

62 *Gold Coast (Constitution) Order in Council, 1950.* There is a handy summary of this and lesser constitutional instruments in *Colonial Reports: Gold Coast, 1950* (London: H.M.S.O., 1952). See also *Gold Coast: Statement by His Majesty's Government on the Report of the Committee on Constitutional Reform,* Colonial No. 250 (London: H.M.S.O., 1949).

63 *Watson Report,* Colonial No. 231, 1948, paras. 31–59, 87–96.

64 The airfield at Takoradi was developed by the R.A.F. and that at Accra by the U.S. during 1940–43 as essential bases for the reinforcement route to the Middle East.

   The social influence of American servicemen in particular, manifested in such externals as clothing, dance music, and beer drinking, was considerable.

65 President Wilson's Fourteen Points had had a comparable, though less drastic, influence *c.* 1918–20, especially on the National Congress of West Africa.

66 An important factor in this gulf was the segregation, begun early

in the twentieth century, on sanitary grounds, of European residential accommodation from the indigenous towns.

67 See David E. Apter, *The Gold Coast in Transition* (Princeton: University Press, 1955), p. 22, n. 8. For a summary of Danquah's views on the connection with ancient Ghana, see his article "The Akan Claim to Origin from Ghana," *West African Review*, XXVI (November and December, 1955), 963–70 and 1107–11, especially p. 1111.

68 See Nkrumah's revealing autobiography, *Ghana* (London: Nelson, 1957), p. 87.

69 See on this point, J. G. Amamoo, *The New Ghana* (London: Pan Books, 1958), p. 20. This is a stimulating account by a young Ghanaian of the period 1948–57.

70 See J. H. Price, *The Gold Coast Election* ("West African Affairs Series No. 11" [London: Bureau of Current Affairs, n.d.]); also the account in *Colonial Reports: Gold Coast, 1951* (London: H.M.S.O., 1952), App. I.

71 Nkrumah's appreciation of the coöperation he had received from Arden-Clarke and the British was signified by the appointment of Sir Charles as Governor-General for the first six months of the life of the new dominion of Ghana. This was an impressive tribute, because whereas the governor of a British *colony* is chosen by and is wholly responsible to the Secretary of State for the Colonies in Britain, the governor-general of a *dominion* is wholly a constitutional head of the state, chosen by the dominion's own government for appointment by the Queen in her capacity not of Queen of the United Kingdom, but as Queen of the dominion in question, and he is unable to act except on the advice of the dominion cabinet. The second Governor-General of Ghana, the Earl of Listowel, a former Labour Secretary of State for India, was also British-born, but in the not inconsiderable interim between Arden-Clarke's departure and Listowel's arrival, the Ghanaian Chief Justice, Sir Arku Korsah, acted as Governor-General and has since done so when Lord Listowel has been absent from the country. Listowel's successor as head of the state will certainly be an African. It is the declared policy of the C.P.P. government that Ghana will shortly become a republic, though, as the case of India has shown, such a change is still compatible with membership of the British Commonwealth.

72 For Nkrumah's account of these years, see his *Ghana*, p. 137 onwards; for Arden-Clarke's, see his lecture "Eight Years of Transition in Ghana," *African Affairs*, LVII, No. 226 (January, 1958), 29–37. For a general account, see Amamoo, *New Ghana*.

Index

Aborigines' Rights Protection Society: origin, 77; political aims, 77–78; and Casely Hayford, 80

Achimota College: foundation and purpose of, 79

Adangme, The: location and origins, 23–24

Aggrey, J. E. K.: vice-principal of Achimota, 79, 112 n53

Akan languages: location, 23; traditions and early history of peoples speaking, 24–29

Akim: gold mines, 53

Akwamu: rise and fall, 52–53; influence on Ashanti, 54

Al Bakri: Muslim geographer, 32

Almoravids: apogee of Berber history, 12; and ancient Ghana, 15, 17

Anokye, Okomfo: Ashanti high priest, 54

Arabs: conquests of Egypt and Maghrib by compared, 11–12. *See also* Islam

Arden-Clarke, Sir Charles: last governor of Gold Coast, 84–85

Ashanti: British rule established in, 4, 65; early trade with, 19–20; rise of, 52, 53–55; Golden Stool of, 54; invasions of Fante by, 55, 59–61, 71, 75; relations with Europeans, 59–61, 71, 73; invaded by the British, 64; defeated in 1826, 71; and opposition to C.P.P., 85

Azambuja, Diego da: builds Elmina castle, 43; opposition to, 49

116